Caroline
The Unhappy Queen

Lord Russell of Liverpool

ᏪᏪᏪᏪᏪᏪᏪᏪᏪᏪᏪᏪᏪᏪᏪᏪᏪᏪᏪ

Caroline
The Unhappy Queen

ᏪᏪᏪᏪᏪᏪᏪᏪᏪᏪᏪᏪᏪᏪᏪᏪᏪᏪᏪ

South Brunswick and New York:
A. S. Barnes and Company

Contents

Illustrations

ᠭᠥᠨᠭᠥᠨᠭᠥᠨᠭᠥᠨᠭᠥᠨᠭᠥᠨᠭᠥᠨᠭᠥᠨᠭᠥᠨᠭᠥᠨᠭᠥᠨᠭᠥᠨᠭᠥᠨ

The portrait of Mrs. Fitzherbert was supplied by
the Mansell Collection. The other illustrations were
supplied by the Radio Times Hulton Picture Library.

Acknowledgements

ରେଏରେଏରେଏରେଏରେଏରେଏରେଏରେଏରେଏରେଏରେଏରେଏରେଏରେଏରେଏରେଏରେଏରେ

I am most grateful to Her Majesty the Queen for graciously giving me permission to make use of material from the Royal Archives.

I also wish to express my thanks to Mr. S. S. Wilson, C.B.E., Keeper of Public Records, for giving me access to certain documents; to Mr. C. S. D. Dobson, Librarian to the House of Lords, for helping me with the research into the parliamentary debates on the Bill of Pains and Penalties and to Sir Charles Petrie Bart for allowing me to quote from *The Life of George Canning* and *The Modern British Monarchy*.

As usual my thanks are due to my wife for the ungrateful task of typing out the manuscript and for much other help and advice during the writing of the book.

ONE

A Marriage of Convenience

ભ્ય૭ભ્ય૭ભ્ય૭ભ્ય૭ભ્ય૭ભ્ય૭ભ્ય૭ભ્ય૭ભ્ય૭ભ્ય૭ભ્ય૭ભ્ય૭ભ્ય૭ભ્ય૭ભ્ય૭

"I SHALL never marry," the Prince of Wales, later to become the Prince Regent and subsequently George IV, once said to the first Earl of Malmesbury. He did not think that he was suited to a marriage of convenience and who would contradict him. In the end it was only the combination of overwhelming debts and the need for a legitimate grandchild to George III which drove him into a marriage which, from the outset, had little chance of success.

Although his future bride appears to have been moderately good-looking she had no other physical attractions. Her mother, the Princess Augusta, was a coarse woman with a vulgar mind and the daughter's underclothes were said to be as filthy as her mother's follies. "I knew," wrote Lord Malmesbury, though he did not explain how he got the information, "that she wore coarse petticoats, coarse shifts and thread stockings and these were never well washed or changed often enough." Nor was that all, there was madness on both sides of her family.

But whatever the truth may have been about the Princess's personal cleanliness, and in the eighteenth century this did not count for very much, she had been in her youth, and continued to be in later life despite her many detractors, an attractive, lively and engaging personality.

Indeed had she never married her dissolute husband, who was to become her evil genius, and had accepted one of the several offers of marriage which she had received before George III selected her as his daughter-in-law, life could not conceivably have turned out to be more tragic than it did.

Her father, Charles William, Duke of Brunswick and husband of George III's sister, the Princess Augusta, adored his daughter and spoiled her. She, in her turn, always remembered him with love and admiration, but with awe, as well she might for he was no ordinary man. "My father," she used to say, "was a hero: they married me to a zero."

There could, however, never have been any reasonable possibility that the marriage of this rather frivolous and irresponsible young girl to such a useless and selfish degenerate as the Prince of Wales would ever be successful. The kindest thing that could be said of him was that he was not the marrying sort. Thackeray's assessment of him was much less charitable.

This George, what was he? I look through all his life and recognize but a bow and a grin. I try to take him to pieces and find silk stockings, padding, stays, a coat with frogs and a fur collar, a star and a blue ribbon, a pocket handkerchief prodigiously scented, one of Truefitt's best nutty brown wigs reeking with oil, and a black stock under waistcoats, more underwaistcoats and then nothing.[1]

It could be said that Thackeray's summing-up failed to mention any of the Prince's good qualities, if indeed there were any, but an estimate of his character, made a hundred years later by an objective historian, does not put him in a more favourable light:

He was a clever versatile lazy man ... attractive and rude by turns,

[1] *The Four Georges* by William Makepeace Thackeray.

but always a liar, always selfish, bad in his private and public conduct and without the least understanding of his age. He was a fair judge of character and could turn a pleasant phrase, but he never concerned himself with anything which did not ultimately affect his own pleasure. . . . He was a poor argument for his own cause and the English Monarchy could hardly have survived a successor of his kind. It may be said that he showed in his private life signs of his father's madness[1] and that in his selfishness and low behaviour he was no worse than four of his six brothers. It is difficult to find other arguments in his favour.[2]

Nevertheless, although nothing can excuse the way in which he treated his wife, his upbringing and the circumstances of his youth were partly responsible for his decadent character. He had feared and hated his grandmother and no one was more pleased than he was when she died. He also hated both his parents and disliked on principle everything which his father enjoyed. George III's chief hobby was agriculture, on account of which he earned the nickname of Farmer George, but the Prince preferred the city lights, and when, at the age of eighteen, he was given a little freedom he seized it with both hands. His father was a Tory, so George became a Whig.

He had never been allowed to mix with other children so he had no companions of his own class, but when he was allowed to set up a home of his own in Buckingham House he was introduced to the wrong people by his uncle the Duke of Cumberland, who "found a satisfaction in turning the Prince's apartments into a combined gambling den, pawnshop and brothel."[3]

---

[1] He had a mania for hoarding hardly less strong than his love of extravagant spending. He kept all his coats, boots and pantaloons over a period of fifty years. After his death bundles of love-letters, women's gloves and locks of hair were found amongst his papers. He also left banknotes scattered in five hundred pocket-books, about £10,000 of loose money in his boxes.

[2] *The Age of Reform* (*The Oxford History of England*) by E. L. Woodward.

[3] *Charles James Fox*, by Drinkwater.

When he was but seventeen years old, Perdita, the actress whose maiden name was Mary Darby, became his mistress. She was four years older than her lover and had been married since 1774, when she was only sixteen years of age, to a waster named Robinson who neglected her and led a life of dissipation which soon landed him in a debtor's prison. Perdita, who by this time had given birth to a child, kept things going by doing any kind of menial job which came her way. Through David Garrick, who had taken some interest in the girl before her marriage, she made her debut on the stage at Drury Lane in the part of Juliet, with William Brereton as Romeo. She became a star on the first night and, but for her appearance before the Prince of Wales at a command performance of *The Winter's Tale*, almost exactly three years later, she would, undoubtedly, have had a successful career on the stage. The Prince, however, fell madly for her and the young woman foolishly deserted the stage and became his mistress. In less than eighteen months, however, he had found a new one and Mrs. Robinson was paid £5,000 for handing over the passionate love letters which the Prince had written to her over the signature of Florizel, and given a life pension of £5,000 a year, which she continued to draw until her untimely death fifteen years later at the early age of forty.

A year after he had rid himself of Perdita the Prince came of age and established himself at Carlton House, where he continued to live a life of dissipation aided and abetted by Charles James Fox and a number of other Whig politicians. As Sir Edward Parry has written:

One wonders how men like Fox, Burke and Sheridan could associate with such a character as George, Prince of Wales. But politics make us acquainted with strange bedfellows. . . . He treated his political friends as he treated the women he ruined to give him pleasure, but grave statesmen should not have been seduced by his advances and one cannot grieve over their betrayal. In the same way some of the Court ladies who sought for his patronage had full warning of the price they would pay for it and one can pass over their stories of neglect and desertion without wasting pity on them.

His meeting with Maria Fitzherbert, however, was something much more serious. He was then twenty-two and she was about twenty-eight. As far as it was possible for him to love anybody the Prince loved Mrs. Fitzherbert, but when a rumour came to the ears of Fox that his royal friend was considering marriage with her he became greatly alarmed and wrote a long letter in which he tried to dissuade the Prince from doing anything so foolish and dangerous.

In a short reply written on the following day, the Prince assured Fox that he need have no fears as there was no truth in the rumour. "Believe me," he wrote, "the world will soon be convinced that there not only is not, but never was, any ground for these reports which of late have been so malevolently circulated."

Nevertheless four days later the Prince and Maria were married according to the rites of the Church of England in the drawing room of her house in Park Street, Mayfair.[1]

How long the Prince would have continued living with Mrs. Fitzherbert, had it not been that by 1794 he was hopelessly in debt, it was impossible to say, but there is reason to suppose that before then he had already begun to tire of her and had started an intrigue with Lady Jersey. In June of that year, however, Mrs. Fitzherbert received a curt note from the Prince that he would never enter her house again.

Two months later the King was delighted to be able to write to William Pitt and give him the good news that he had long been waiting to receive:

I have this a.m. seen the Prince of Wales who has acquainted me with his having broken off all connection with Mrs. Fitzherbert and his

[1] The marriage certificate is in the Royal Archives at Windsor Castle.

desire of entering into a more creditable line of life by marrying, expressing at the same time that his wish is that a niece of the Princess of Brunswick is the person. Undoubtedly she is the person who naturally must be the most agreeable to me. I expressed my approbation of the idea, provided his plan was to lead to a life that would make him appear respectable and consequently render the Princess happy. He assured me that he perfectly coincided with me in my opinion. I then said that until Parliament assembled no arrangement could be taken except by sounding my sister that no idea of any other marriage may be encouraged.

For the King to have told Pitt that it was the Prince's wish that he should marry Caroline was, perhaps, putting it a little too strongly. The only other bride considered eligible was Princess Louise of Mecklenberg-Strelitz, but the Prince would not entertain the idea of marrying her although his mother tried to persuade him. His decision in favour of Caroline, however, appears to have been a question of Hobson's choice, for his private opinion on the subject is said to have been, "one damned German *frau* is as good as another." One of his friends believed that Lady Jersey may have had a hand in influencing his choice, for Princess Louise was the better-looking of the two and, had the Prince of Wales married her, Lady Jersey's position as one of his mistresses might more easily have been in jeopardy.

Having informed Pitt of the Prince's welcome decision the King lost no time, and, on 14th November, Lord Malmesbury, who was already in Germany on a special mission to the Court of Berlin, received instructions to demand the hand of the Princess Caroline of Brunswick for his son. He was given no discretion whatsoever but it is clear from the entries in his diaries that, while publicly he confined himself strictly to carrying out His Majesty's command, in private he did all he could to prepare the rather wilful and independent girl for what was to come.

On his arrival in Brunswick a fortnight later he was immediately asked by the Duke and Duchess to dine with them so that he should have the earliest opportunity of meeting the Princess. At dinner he sat next to his hostess, but when not actually engaged in conversation with her he appears to have wasted no time and kept the Princess under a watchful eye, for he wrote a detailed description of her in his diary before he retired to bed. "She appeared," he wrote, "to be much embarrassed when I was presented to her but during the evening she gave every indication that she was vastly happy with her future expectations." She had "a pretty face not expressive of softness," and although "she did not have a graceful figure she had a good bust and *des épaules impertinentes.*"[1]

Her mother talked of nothing else but the offer of marriage and was delighted at the prospect, though for the wrong reason. All the German princesses, she told Malmesbury, had learnt English in the hope of becoming Princess of Wales, but she had never imagined that the choice would fall on her daughter because she knew that her brother, King George III, was against marriages between first cousins.

As the days went by, during which time Malmesbury had several long conversations with the Duke of Brunswick on another subject, his opinion of Caroline changed for the better. He found that she improved on acquaintance and was "gay, cheerful and sensible." On 3rd December, the day fixed for the final interview before the signing of the marriage treaty, a letter arrived from the Prince of Wales enclosing a portrait of himself and precise instructions to leave for England with the Princess as soon as possible. On the following morning the treaty was signed and a dinner and ball were held that evening to celebrate the occasion.

The instructions which the Prince had given Malmesbury by letter were in flat contradiction to those which he had received

[1] *Diaries and correspondence of James Harris, First Earl of Malmesbury*, edited by his grandson, 1844.

from the King. Nevertheless, Malmesbury wrote to the Prince to the effect that he and his charge would set out for England on the 11th, provided that before then he received confirmation that the fleet which was to escort them across the channel had already sailed. But it was not to be. Nearly four months were to elapse before the Princess and her escort entered the Thames and anchored off Gravesend.

During this time the Princess had many talks with Lord Malmesbury about the future and received a lot of sound advice which she appears to have taken without offence. On several occasions, also, both the Duke and his mistress, Mademoiselle Hertzfeldt, warned Malmesbury about the Princess's faults, such as they were. They amounted, however, to little more than indiscretion and a habit of saying too much at the wrong time. Caroline, the Duke said, was not difficult but, perhaps, a little lacking in judgment. "Try and persuade her," he told Malmesbury, "not to be free in giving opinions of persons and things aloud." All this was confirmed by Mademoiselle Hertzfeldt. Caroline had to be dealt with strictly as she was inclined to be tactless and lose her temper. Some guidance should be given her as to her behaviour after her arrival in England, and, in Mademoiselle Hertzfeldt's opinion, Lord Malmesbury would be the most suitable person to give it. He took the hint and advised Caroline, "to avoid familiarity, to have no confidantes, to avoid giving any opinion, to approve but not to admire excessively, and to be perfectly silent on politics and party." She took all this in good part and hoped that Lord Malmesbury would continue to advise her after she reached England.

Eventually, on Easter Sunday 1795, the Princess disembarked at Greenwich about noon. The royal coaches had not yet arrived since one of the ladies-in-waiting, Lady Jersey, had delayed the start, doubtless deliberately, by not being ready in time. When, at last, she did arrive Lady Jersey professed herself as being "very much dissatisfied with the Princess's mode of dress," and expressed herself in such terms that Lord Malmesbury thought it his duty to speak "rather sharply" to her. She also said that she could not sit in a coach with her back to the horses and hoped that she might be allowed to sit facing them. Lord Malmesbury told her in no uncertain terms that this was strictly forbidden by the King, and that as she must have known that riding backwards in a coach disagreed with her, she ought never to have accepted the appointment of a Lady of the Bedchamber, who ought never to sit forward, and that if she was likely to be sick he would put Mrs. Aston into the coach with the Princess. That did the trick, and Lady Jersey and Mrs. Harcourt, who had accompanied the Princess on her journey across the channel, "sat backwards and the Princess sat by herself forward." After these unpleasant preliminaries the cortège eventually reached the Duke of Cumberland's apartments in Cleveland Row at about half past two.

The King and the Prince of Wales were at once informed of Caroline's arrival and the Prince came to meet her. What happened then is best described in Lord Malmesbury's own words.

I, according to the established etiquette, introduced (no one else being in the room) the Princess Caroline to him. She, very properly, in consequence of my saying to her it was the right way of proceeding, attempted to kneel to him. He raised her (gracefully enough) and embraced her, said barely one word, turned round, retired to a distant part of the appartment, and, calling me to him, said, "Harris I am not well; pray get me a glass of brandy." I said, "Sir had you not better have a glass of water?"—upon which he, much out of humour, said with an oath, "No: I will go directly to the Queen," and away he went. The Princess, left alone during this short moment, was in a state of astonishment; and on my joining her, said, "Je le trouve très gros, et nullement aussi beau que son portrait." ("I find him very fat and not half as handsome as his portrait.")

Caroline can hardly be blamed for being somewhat astonished.

She had heard a good deal about the Prince, including much to his discredit, but this was more than she had expected. His callous rudeness was still first and foremost in her mind at dinner when her behaviour disgusted the Prince and was the beginning of a dislike which soon developed into hatred.

Three days later, in the Chapel Royal, St. James's, the wedding took place at eight o'clock in the evening with all the appropriate pomp and circumstance, but it was obvious to anyone who had eyes to see that it was a marriage in name only—indeed on the previous day many bets were taken at all the leading West End clubs that it would never take place. The Prince arrived, apparently drunk, though his state may have been due more to the state of nervous apprehension he was in than the amount of drink which he had taken, although this was more than was good for him. Whatever may have been the Princess's feelings after the shock of the first meeting with her future husband she managed to disguise them, and chatted happily with the Duke of Clarence while waiting at the altar for the Prince's arrival. Throughout the ceremony she conducted herself with complete decorum but he behaved most strangely and on one occasion he suddenly rose from his knees and looked anxiously around as though he was going to make a bolt for it. The King quickly left his place, went up to his son and told him to kneel down again.

The obvious tension was not relieved when the Archbishop of Canterbury paused while reading the passage, calling upon any persons who knew any just impediment why these two persons should not be joined together in holy matrimony to say so or forever hold their peace, and looked intently at the King and the Prince of Wales. It is more than likely that he had heard rumours of the Prince's marriage to Mrs. Fitzherbert, but in that event only two proper courses were open to him: either to refuse to conduct the ceremony of marriage or to gabble through the dangerous injunction and hope that nothing embarrassing would happen.

Luckily nothing did, and the service ended without incident and the guests went to Buckingham House for the reception, which was later followed by a family supper party. What happened after that is wrapped in mystery, and perhaps it is better so, but Caroline, later describing the wedding night to Lady Bury, told her that the Prince spent it "sleeping under the grate where he fell and where I left him."

Somewhere, sometime during the night, however, it would appear that the Prince managed to consummate the marriage despite his condition—although there were many rumours, though no real evidence, to the contrary—for in nine months' time almost to the day Caroline gave birth to a girl, the unhappy Princess Charlotte. Early next morning the newly weds were heard shouting at each other in the Princess's room, the door was flung open and the Prince, mad with anger and still fully dressed but dishevelled, rushed out and disappeared into his own room.

Two days later they both went to Windsor and from there to Kempshott, a house in Hampshire which had previously belonged to Mrs. Fitzherbert. To take his new wife, the future Queen of England, to spend her honeymoon in the house which had previously belonged to his former mistress and morganatic wife was bad enough, but that was not the only insult she had to bear. Lady Jersey stayed with them, and the Prince when he was not with her spent the rest of the time drinking and gambling with some of his most dissolute friends.

During the first few weeks after their return to Carlton House Lord Malmesbury dined with them frequently. It was hardly surprising in the circumstances that the Princess's behaviour on some of these occasions was not all that could be desired. She had no friends at Court whatsoever and could hardly be blamed for having little or no consideration for her husband's feelings. After one of these dinners at which the Prince of Orange was a guest the Prince of Wales took Malmesbury aside and asked him what he thought of Caroline's behaviour. He admitted that it left much to be desired but told the Prince that the Duke of Brunswick had warned him about it and had told him that she had been brought up very strictly and that it was necessary *de la tenir serrée*. To this the Prince replied that he could see it "but too plainly; but why Harris did you not tell me before or write to me from Brunswick?" Malmesbury said that what the Duke had said was only intended as a friendly warning and that it did not cast "any real slur or aspersion on the Princess." The reason why he had not informed the Prince about this by letter, Malmesbury said, was that he had not been sent to Brunswick "on a discretionary commission, but with the most positive commands to ask Princess Caroline in marriage and nothing more." Nevertheless, he continued, "had I discovered notorious or glaring defects or such as were of a nature to render the union unseemly, I should have felt it as a bounden duty to have stated them but it must have been to the King and to no one else." The Prince seemed to understand this, although with bad grace.

During the next few months there was to be no respite for poor Caroline. In June 1795, only two months after the marriage had taken place, the House of Commons was asked to increase the Prince's allowance to £125,000 per annum, and a Royal Commission was set up to liquidate his debts, which by then amounted to no less than £639,890. It is not surprising that the King told Lord Eldon, the Lord Chancellor, that he felt sure that he would be the last King of England.

It was bad enough for Caroline to realize that the sole reason for her marriage was that the Prince of Wales should settle down to a respectable married life in order that the British Parliament might be persuaded to liquidate the debts of the heir to the throne. Had there been any chance that the marriage would be a happy one this cross might not have been so hard to bear, but she was now tied for the rest of her life to a worthless despicable husband. As she told Lady Charlotte Bury, one of her ladies-in-waiting: "Judge what it is to have a drunken husband on one's wedding day and one who spent the greater part of his bridal night under the grate where he fell and where I left him. If anybody were to say to me at this moment, will you live your life all over again or be killed, I would choose death, for you know sooner or later we must all die, but to live a life of wretchedness twice over—oh, *mein Gott*, no!"

Meanwhile she awaited the birth of her child with mixed feelings which she laid bare in a letter that she wrote to a friend of hers in Germany on 1st December 1795.

I expect speedily to be the mother of an infant. I know not how I shall be able to support myself in the hour of solitude but I trust in the benevolence of Heaven. The Queen seldom visits me and my sisters-in-law are equally attentive. Yet the English character I admire, and when I appear in public nothing can be more flattering than the reception which I meet with. I am surrounded with miserable and evil principles: and whatever I attempt is misrepresented. The Countess[1] still continues here. I hate her and I am confident that she does me no less. My husband is very partial to her and so the rest you will be able to divine.

On 7th January 1796 the child was born amid general rejoicing. Even the Prince of Wales was delighted, not because of any fatherly feelings towards his daughter but because he felt that he had fulfilled his part of the bargain by presenting the nation with an heir to the throne and would henceforth be free to live his own life without having to show, even in public, any consideration for his wife. He lost no time in letting her know this, and sent a message to Lord Cholmondley to the effect that he intended to have nothing more to do with her. She told the bearer of this message that she was not prepared to accept a verbal dismissal and

[1] The Countess of Jersey.

that her husband must put his decision in writing and that if there were to be a separation it must be final. To this he was only too ready to agree and wrote accordingly. Caroline replied on the 6th May as follows:

The avowal of your conversation with Lord Cholmondeley neither surprises nor offends me; it merely confirmed what you have tacitly insinuated for this twelve months. But after this it would be a want in delicacy, or rather an unworthy meanness in me, were I to complain of these conditions which you impose upon yourself. I should have returned no answer to your letter if it had not been conceived in terms to make it doubtful whether this arrangement proceeds from you or from me; and you are aware that the honour of it belongs to you alone.

The letter which you announce to me as the last, obliged me to communicate to the King, as to my sovereign and my father, both your avowal and my answer. You will find enclosed the copy of my letter to the King. I apprise you of it that I may not merit the slightest reproach of duplicity from you. As I have, at this moment, no protection but His Majesty I refer myself solely to him upon this subject; and if my conduct meet his approbation I shall be in some degree, at least, consoled. I retain every sentiment of gratitude for the situation in which I find myself, as Princess of Wales, enabled by your means to indulge in the free exercise of a virtue dear to my heart—I mean charity. It will be my duty to act upon another motive—that of giving an example of patience and resignation under every trial. Do me the justice to believe that I shall never cease to pray for your happiness and to be

Your much devoted
Caroline.

Thus did their marriage come to an end, except in name only, and she can have had no genuine regrets that it was over. From the very first night it had been sheer purgatory. She had been living most of the time under the same roof as one of her husband's mistresses in whose presence and in the presence of many of his friends she was constantly and degradingly humiliated. In his *Memoirs of George the Fourth* Huish gave this description of life in Carlton House:

> It may be looked upon, at this time as a Pandora box filled with treachery and vice. The immediate associates of the Prince, male and female, were persons distinguished for their immorality of conduct, their licentiousness and debauchery. Scenes of the most indecent nature were daily and nightly practised under its roof which, as it was now the residence of a virtuous wife and mother, ought to have been uncontaminated by the presence of the harlot or libertine.

When she complained of what went on to the Queen she was merely told that the Prince had every right to choose his own friends and that it was a constant embarrassment to him that his wife lived with him in London. No wonder Caroline loathed her mother-in-law.

The King, however, who was Caroline's uncle as well as her father-in-law, was extremely upset at his son's treatment of her, and did all he could to maintain the rights to which she was entitled as Charlotte's mother. As he wrote to Lord Eldon, "Caroline's injuries deserve the utmost attention of the King as her own conduct has proved irreproachable." He prevailed upon the Prince to allow Charlotte to remain under her mother's care and this she did until after her eighth birthday.

TWO

Montague House

ତଵ

IN 1797 the Princess of Wales was made to leave Carlton House and eventually to live at Montague House, Blackheath, where she remained until she decided to go abroad in 1814. While living there she became acquainted with Sir John and Lady Douglas, who were frequent visitors. It was through this meeting that the Delicate Investigation came about, an inquiry made by a tribunal composed of a number of the Prince of Wales' friends into his wife's conduct, acting upon a scandalous report made to the Prince by Lady Douglas and her husband in December 1805.

The news of the Princess's separation from her husband soon became general knowledge and the reaction of the people in London was most sympathetic. Wherever she appeared in public she was greeted with cheers and on her first visit to Covent Garden Opera House the whole audience gave her a standing ovation. Something else also happened which must have given her considerable satisfaction, the dismissal of Lady Jersey, whose only comment was that the Prince was a "sequence; King, Queen and Knave." While he was still living with Caroline he had wanted his mistress under the same roof, not that he really cared much for her, but for the purpose of outraging his wife. Now that they had parted all he wanted was that Mrs. Fitzherbert should return to him. Eventually he got his way, but not until she had obtained a ruling from the Pope, of which, incidentally, His Holiness kept no record, that Mrs. Fitzherbert was the Prince's lawful wife and that his marriage to Caroline was not legal.

Once Caroline was installed at Montague House she soon settled down to a more normal life and entertained a large number of friends, although all those who regularly visited her there well knew that by so doing they would lose the goodwill and the patronage of their future King. This does not appear to have worried them unduly, however, for the Prince was generally regarded with loathing and contempt, except by some of his Whig cronies, and there was always the possibility that his excesses would remove him from the scene before he could succeed his father. Lawyers, artists and writers were all frequent guests of the Princess, as well as statesmen and politicians. The Queen and her daughters never visited Caroline but the King often did. Her daughter, Charlotte, was not allowed to live with her, having been moved to Windsor on the Prince's orders. She was, however, allowed to visit her mother once a week.

A German writer, Herr Campe, who, incidentally, translated Daniel Defoe's *Robinson Crusoe* into German, visited the Princess in 1802 and in a book entitled *Travels in England* described the life she led there, and, in particular, the charitable work which was her main occupation. When he was at Montague House one of the things which his hostess showed him with great pride was her large vegetable garden. "This," she said, "is my principal concern. Here I endeavour to acquire the honourable name of a farmer and that, as you see, not merely in jest. The vegetables which I raise here in considerable quantity are carried to town and sold. The produce amounts annually to a handsome sum." But it was the purpose to which this handsome sum was applied which most interested Herr Campe. The Princess "had no court, no officers of state, no chamberlains, and no maids of honour because she had no occasion for them," nor was the money used to educate her daughter or for her own personal expenses but "to educate eight or nine poor orphan children to whom she had the condescension to supply the place of a mother. Her own was the child of the State and, according to the constitution of the country, must not, alas, be educated by herself. These poor children, on the other hand, were boarded by her with honest people in the neighbourhood." Herr Campe then described the charming and affecting scene when the Princess introduced some of her foster children to him. "They seemed," he wrote, "perfectly ignorant of the high rank of their foster mother . . . the sight of a stranger somewhat abashed them but their bashfulness soon wore off and they appeared to be perfectly at home." With her they behaved quite naturally. "People find fault with me," Caroline said, "for not doing more for these children after I have taken them under my care. I ought, in their opinion, to provide them with more elegant and costly clothes . . . but I only laugh at their censure for I know what I am about. It is not my intention to raise these children to a rank superior to that in which they are placed: in that rank I mean them to remain and to become useful, virtuous and happy members of society. The boys are destined to become expert seamen and the girls skilful, sensible, industrious housewives, nothing more."

This charitable work which so impressed Herr Campe was unfortunately soon to land the Princess in a great deal of trouble, for her newly acquired friends, the Douglases, were to become her bitterest enemies.

One of the children who had been introduced to Herr Campe on the occasion of his visit to Montague House was William Austin, who had been born in the Brownlow Street Hospital on 11th July 1802. His father, Samuel Austin, was a dockyard labourer, and as the family were extremely poor the Princess took interest in them and eventually decided to adopt the baby William. The child was brought to live at Montague House where his mother came and saw him whenever she liked. Caroline, however, became very fond of William and treated him just as she would her own child. That was the truth, the whole truth, and nothing but the truth, but in 1806 the Prince of Wales, who since their separation had never ceased spying on his wife in order to discredit her and hold her up to calumny, submitted evidence to a Commission consisting of Lord Erskine, who was then the Lord Chancellor; Lord Grenville, the First Lord of the Treasury; Lord Spencer, Secretary of State; and Lord Ellenborough, that Austin was, in fact, the illegitimate son of the Princess.

Sir John and Lady Douglas, who came to live in Blackheath in 1801, were very friendly with Admiral Sir William Sidney Smith, under whom Sir John had previously served, and just before his departure for Italy and Sicily on an important mission for which he had been specially selected by Nelson, Sir Sidney was living with the Douglases. The Admiral, who was very good company and never stopped talking, principally about himself, was a frequent visitor to Montague House and having been introduced to the Princess of Wales by the Douglases became a great favourite there and she never tired of listening to his rambling reminiscences.[1]

Lady Douglas was of humble origin, being the child of a private soldier and of the illegitimate daughter of a Bath lawyer, and she was, doubtless, flattered when she got to know the Princess and began to be invited with her husband to many of the parties given at Montague House. It later came to the Princess's knowledge, however, that Lady Douglas had said some scandalous things about her and she sent word that in future she would no longer be *persona grata* in the Princess's home. This was very unwise of her as

---

[1] See *Knight of the Sword* by the author, 1964.

she had been warned by many of her friends that Lady Douglas was a dangerous vindictive woman and would leave no stone unturned to try and damage Caroline's reputation. This warning proved to be only too true.

The Douglases, incensed by the ultimatum from Montague House, began a campaign of slander against the unfortunate Princess, who consulted her brother-in-law, the Duke of Kent. A year later the Prince learned of the Duke's visit to Caroline, sent for him, and was then told the whole story. About twelve months ago, the Duke said, he had received a note from the Princess requesting him to visit her at Blackheath in order to assist her in arranging a difficult matter between her, Sir Sidney Smith, and the Douglases, the details of which she would inform him when he called to see her. The Princess told him at their interview that she supposed he knew that for some years she had been on quite friendly terms with Charlotte Douglas but that later she had intimated through a Mrs. Vernon, one of her Ladies, that Lady Douglas's presence at Montague House would no longer be welcome. This had resulted in her receiving a request in the joint names of Sir Sidney, Sir John and Lady Douglas for an audience to demand an explanation of what they considered to be an unwarranted affront.

The Princess, not wishing to be personally involved, had asked the Duke to intervene on her behalf and to take whatever steps he judged best to put an end to the matter. The Duke told her that as he knew neither Sir John nor his wife he could not, in the first instance, address himself to them but, as he knew Sir Sidney slightly, he would, if she agreed, approach him and see whether the affair could be amicably settled. Eventually he saw the Admiral, who told him of the real reason why an audience with the Princess of Wales had been requested. The Douglases had received, Sir Sidney told the Duke, a most scandalous anonymous letter which, from the handwriting and style, Sir John and he were both convinced had been written by the Princess herself. The contents of the letter were not, at this interview, disclosed, though they were later. Knowing, however, the unfortunate effect which the disclosure of this information would have if the facts became public, and the use to which the Prince of Wales would enthusiastically put it, for his own spiteful purposes, the Duke urged Sir Sidney to persuade the Douglases to take no further action and let the matter drop. The Admiral said that it would not be too easy to persuade Sir John to do this but that he would do his best.

A few days later Sir Sidney called on the Duke and told him that he, personally, would do nothing further but that the only promise he had been able, with great difficulty, to extract from Sir John amounted to no more than that "he would under existing circumstances remain quiet if left unmolested but he could not pledge himself not to bring the subject forward hereafter when the same motive might no longer operate to keep him silent."

It did not take Sir John long, however, to break his promise, for soon afterwards he and his wife signed a statement which was eventually handed to the Prince of Wales and formed the basis of the allegations which the Commission were asked to investigate. This document, which was headed "Statement of Lady Douglas" and consisted of more than 20,000 words, was of a most scandalous and defamatory nature and covered the entire period of the Douglases' acquaintanceship with the Princess. The two most serious allegations which it contained, however, concerned the anonymous letter which Sir Sidney had mentioned in his first interview with the Duke of Kent and the entirely false accusation that William Austin was, in fact, the illegitimate child of the Princess of Wales.

It is abundantly clear that Lady Douglas's statement was made at the request of the Prince, probably as a result of information which he had received from the Duke of Sussex who had heard some of the rumours which Charlotte Douglas had been studiously spreading around. He sent for the Douglases, listened to what they had to say with evident relish, and asked them to put it all on paper and "not to spare the horses."

His Royal Highness [the statement begins], having judged proper to order me to detail to him, as heir apparent, the whole circumstances of my acquaintance with Her Royal Highness the Princess of Wales from the day I first spoke with her to the present time, I felt it my duty, as a subject, to comply without hesitation with His Royal Highness's commands: and I did so because I conceived, even putting aside the rights of an heir-apparent, he was justified in informing himself as to the actions of his wife who, from all the information he had collected, seemed so likely to disturb the tranquillity of the country; and it appeared to me that in so doing His Royal Highness evinced his earnest regard for the real interest of the country in endeavouring to prevent such a person from, perhaps, one day placing a spurious heir upon the English throne and which His Royal Highness had a right to fear and communicate to the Sovereign, as the Princess of Wales told me, if she were discovered in bringing her son into the world she would give the Prince of Wales the credit of it, for she had slept two nights in the year she was pregnant in Carlton House. As an English woman, educated in the highest respectful attachment to the royal family; as a daughter of an English officer, who has all his life received the most gracious marks of approbation and protection from His Majesty and from His Royal Highness the Prince of Wales; and as the wife of an officer whom our beloved King had honoured with a public mark of his approbation and who is bound to the Royal family by ties of respectful regard and attachment which nothing can ever brake [*sic*], I feel it my duty to make known the Princess of Wales's sentiments and conduct, now and whenever I may be called upon.

Seldom can such hypocrisy have been put on paper as in the introduction to this statement. Hell knows no fury like a woman scorned and Charlotte Douglas must have derived as much pleasure from writing it as the Prince must have enjoyed reading it. Necessity is said to be the mother of invention but malice can be an even more powerful incentive and in Lady Douglas's statement nothing was left to the imagination. Everything which the Princess said to this woman or in her presence was given a different meaning and twisted in such a way or given out of its context so as to create the impression that she was basically coarse, vulgar, unscrupulous, and completely lacking in morals.

The first intimation she had from the Princess, Lady Douglas wrote, was just after she had been at Montague House at Caroline's request. One evening the Princess arrived at the Douglases' house in great agitation. "I must tell you something," she said to Lady Douglas, "but I am sure you know all the while. I thought you had completely found me out and therefore I came to you . . . I am with child and the child came to life when I was breakfasting with Lady Willoughby. The milk flowed up into my breast so fast that it came through my muslin gown and I was obliged to pretend that I had spilt something and go upstairs to wipe my gown with a napkin."

Lady Douglas said that she hoped the Princess was mistaken as how could she possibly carry such an affair through? No, said Caroline, she was sure of it and these sort of things only require a good courage. "You will be surprised to see how well I manage it and I am determined to suckle the child myself."

It was because she was pregnant, the Princess later explained to Lady Douglas as set out in the signed statement, that she began her charitable work of providing for destitute children whose parents, through poverty, were unable to look after them properly. This was being done as a cover-plan. "When you hear of my having taken children in baskets from poor people," she said, "take no notice: that is the way I mean to manage. I shall take any that offer, and the one I will have will be presented in the same way, which, as I have taken others, will never be thought anything about."

Lady Douglas then asked her how would she be able to conceal the fact of her pregnancy from the outside world and particularly from other members of the royal family, whom she could not avoid meeting from time to time. "That," said Caroline, "would not be difficult." She knew how to manage her dress, and by continually increasing large cushions behind, no one would notice her condition.

A few weeks later, on 13th October, the Douglases received a note from the Princess asking that neither they nor Sir Sidney Smith should visit Montague House for the time being as it was feared that some of the children there had developed measles. From then until her return from Gloucestershire where she had been spending Christmas Lady Douglas never saw the Princess, but on her next visit there was a baby in Caroline's bedroom "asleep on a sofa with a piece of scarlet cloth thrown over her." Here, at last, was the evidence that this evil woman wanted to support what she had been telling everyone for some months past. It is, nevertheless, strange that she could really have believed that her plan to ruin the Princess could succeed. Everyone knew, including all the staff at Montague House, of Caroline's interest in babies and young children as Herr Campe had done. Nor had there been any concealment of the adoption of the Austin baby, it was known to all who were in any way connected with the Princess's household.

Shortly after Lady Douglas's first sight of William Austin she and her husband went to live in Devonshire and it was after their unexpected return to Blackheath, which the Princess had never expected to happen, that the anonymous letter incident arose. Lady Douglas, in her statement, described it in these words:

> I now received by twopenny post a long anonymous letter written by this restless, mischievous person, the Princess of Wales, in which, in language which anyone who had ever heard her speak would have known to be hers, she called me all kinds of names ... such is

the spirit of this foreigner, which would have disgraced a house-maid to have written, and it enclosed a fabricated anonymous letter which she pretends to have received and upon which she builds her doubts and disapprobation of me as it advises her not to trust me, for that I am indiscrete and tell everybody that the child she took from Deptford was her own. The whole construction of both these epistles, from beginning to end, are evidently that of a foreigner, and a very ignorant one and the vulgarity of it is altogether quite shocking.

Lady Douglas showed the letter to her husband and he showed it to Sir Sidney Smith and both of them, according to Lady Douglas, were certain that the Princess had written it, but she had not, apparently, yet done her worst:

Her fury became so unbounded that she sought what she would do most atrociously wicked, and inhuman . . . she made two drawings with a pen and ink and sent them to us by the twopenny post; representing me as having disgraced myself with my husbands' old friend, Sir Sidney Smith. They are of the most indecent nature, drawn with her own hand, and words upon them in her own handwriting. Sir John, Sir Sidney and myself can all swear point blank without a moment's hesitation, and if Her Royal Highness is a subject amenable to the laws of this country (and I conceive her to be so) she ought to be tried and judged by the laws for doing thus, to throw firebrands into the bosom of a quiet family.

Sir John put the drawings into his pocket and went at once to his old friend Sir Sidney who was as much astonished as Sir John was. He swore that the suggestion was a "wicked calomny" and that the handwriting was, indeed, that of the Princess of Wales.

They demanded an immediate interview with Her Royal Highness but received no acknowledgement, whereupon Lady Douglas wrote as follows to the Princess:

Madam,

I received your former anonymous letter safe; also your two last, with drawings.

I am, Madam,

Your obedient servant,

Charlotte Douglas

Lady Douglas ended her statement by declaring that she and her husband were prepared to confirm all the allegations made in it "if this should be required for His Majesty's further information."

THREE

The Delicate Investigation

ᏬᏬᏬᏬᏬᏬᏬᏬᏬᏬᏬᏬᏬᏬᏬᏬᏬᏬᏬᏬᏬᏬᏬᏬᏬᏬ

WHEN the Prince of Wales decided to leave Caroline and return
to Mrs. Fitzherbert he had no intention of letting sleeping dogs lie.
His feeling towards the Princess was not merely one of dislike but
of hatred and revulsion, and he was determined if possible to
humiliate and hurt her. As he read Lady Douglas's statement his
hopes must have been raised and he showed it to Lord Thurlow, a
former Lord Chancellor, and Sir Samuel Romilly, who advised
him to inform the King and to make further inquiries as to whether
the allegations made by Lady Douglas were supported by any
independent evidence. Other statements were obtained from
members of the staff at Montague House and, after studying them
and consulting Thurlow, the King appointed a Commission under
his Royal Warrant "to inquire into the truth of the allegations
accusing the Princess of Wales of guilty intercourse with Sir
Thomas Lawrence, Sir Sidney Smith, Captain Manby and others
and to report thereon." The proceedings of the Delicate Investigation then began.

Robert Huish, in his *Memoirs of George the Fourth*, wrote this
about it:

It is impossible to look back upon the intrigues described, and the character of the actors who played their parts therein, and not form some decided opinion in regard to the number of agents who lent themselves to "this most foul and damnable conspiracy". Men and women of the highest rank; lawyers of eminence; hireling understrappers; even clergymen of honest repute, and the whole of the Prince's Court, without exception, from Lord Moira (who in this business lost "the fame of a thousand years") down to the doorkeeper and the scullery wench, combined to destroy one lone woman, while her husband, rioting in wantonness and voluptuousness, openly or sinisterly encouraged the attacks which had for their end her death on a scaffold. Even the cradle in which her infancy was reared was ransacked for nursery tales, her infancy was slandered, and her puberty corrupted by the inventions of her enemies. By what course of tortuous policy was such a woman selected for the arms of the Prince of Wales? Who advised the connection or what must that man have been who consented to accept it?

The Commission, which for some unexplicable reason held its sittings at 10 Downing Street, opened its proceedings on 1st June 1806 by hearing the evidence of Lady Douglas, when she confirmed in every detail the statement which she had originally made at the request of the Prince of Wales. The first intimation which the Princess received that an official inquiry into her conduct was taking place was when two attorneys arrived at Montague House on the morning of the 7th June with a warrant summoning a number of her household staff to appear before the Commission for examination as witness. They included Frances Lloyd, Mary Ann Wilson, Samuel Roberts, Thomas Stileman, Charlotte Sander and John Sicard. In addition to these witnesses two other members of the household gave evidence, Robert Bidgood and William Cole; the Princess's doctors were also called, and a questionnaire by Lady Willoughby was admitted in evidence.

Bidgood and Cole gave some evidence of having seen Sir Sidney Smith alone with the Princess on a number of occasions quite late at night and Cole said that the Princess had appeared to him to be "too familiar" with the Admiral, but none of the other members of her domestic staff corroborated this evidence in the slightest degree. Sir Sidney was a striking personality and a great conversationalist and the graphic accounts of his campaigns must have brightened up the unfortunate Princess's enforced loneliness. From what has been said of him the gallant Admiral's exploits would have lost none of their glamour in the telling, but once he had opened his mouth it is unlikely that he would have stopped to do anything more sinister.[1]

With regard to the gravest allegation brought against Caroline, namely that she had given birth to a son in Montague House and that William Austin was the child in question, there was not a scintilla of evidence to support what Lady Douglas had told the Commission during her examination.

Bidgood and Cole, whose evidence regarding Sidney Smith was slightly compromising, both stated that they had no reason whatsoever to believe that the Princess was ever in a state of pregnancy. Mary Ann Wilson, who was housemaid to the ladies who attended the Princess, stated that the Princess could not have been "with child" without her knowing it, and the Princess's personal maid, Charlotte Sander, confirmed from her own knowledge that the child, William Austin, was the son of Samuel and Sophia Austin who lived in Deptford and that the baby was brought by the mother to Montague House when he was four months old. The mother identified "Willikins" as her own son and the Registrar of Births produced the entry in the register. The main allegations in Lady Douglas's statement, as repeated in her evidence, were conclusively proved to be a tissue of lies.

Finally the questionnaire which at Lord Spencer's request was put to Lady Willoughby was admitted in evidence. The questions put to her and her replies were as follows:

[1] *Knight of the Sword* by the author, page 115.

Question 1 Does Lady Willoughby remember seeing the Princess of Wales at breakfast or dinner at her house, either at Whitehall or Bechenham on or about the months of May or June 1802?

Answer In the course of the last ten years the Princess of Wales has frequently done me the honour to breakfast and dine at Whitehall and Langley, in Kent. Her Royal Highness may have been at my house in the months of May or June 1802 but at the periods at which I have had the honour of receiving her I have no precise recollection.

Question 2 Has her Ladyship any recollection of the circumstances of Her Royal Highness having retired from the company of such breakfast or dinner on account or under the pretence of having spilt anything over her handkerchief? And if so, did Lady Willoughby attend her Royal Highness on that occasion and what then passed between them relative to the circumstances?

Answer I do not remember Her Royal Highness having at any time retired from the company either at Whitehall, or at Langley, under the pretence of having spilt anything over her handkerchief.

Question 3 Had Lady Willoughby frequent opportunities in the course of that year to see Her Royal Highness, the Princess of Wales and at what periods, and did she at any time during the year observe any appearance which led her to suspect that the Princess was pregnant?

Answer To the best of my remembrance I had few opportunities of seeing the Princess of Wales in the year 1802 and I do not recollect having observed any particular circumstances relative to Her Royal Highness's appearance.

Question 4 Is Lady Willoughby acquainted with any other circumstances leading to the same conclusion, or tending to establish the fact of a criminal intercourse or improper familiarity between Her Royal Highness and any other person whatever, and if so what are they?

Answer During the ten years I have had the honour of knowing the Princess of Wales I do not bear in mind a single instance of Her Royal Highness's conduct in society towards any individual tending to establish the fact of a criminal intercourse or improper familiarity.

In their report to the King the members of the Commission stated that they were happy to declare their perfect conviction that there was no foundation whatever for believing that the child which was then living with the Princess was the child of Her Royal Highness or that she was delivered of a child in the year 1802, nor had anything appeared which could warrant their belief that she was pregnant in that year or at any other period within the scope of their inquiries.

The identity of the child, its parentage, the place and date of its birth, the time and circumstances of its being taken under Her Royal Highness's protection were so established by such a concurrence both of direct and circumstantial evidence as to leave no question of doubt. The child, the report stated, was beyond all doubt born in the Brownlow Street Hospital, on 11th July 1802 of the body of Sophia Austin and was first brought to the Princess's house in the following November. There was no doubt whatsoever about the Princess not having been in a state of pregnancy and the evidence of Lady Douglas on that count was "not entitled to the smallest credit".

With regard to the question of whether the evidence given by four of the witnesses who appeared before the Commission regarding any conduct of Her Royal Highness which, having regard to her exalted rank and station must necessarily give occasion to unfavourable interpretations, should be believed, the report stated that it was not for the members of the Commission to decide, "This was left to His Majesty's wisdom."

The Commission's report, therefore, triumphantly cleared the Princess of all the serious allegations which had been made against her, and in respect of the other suggestions made it placed the ball fairly and squarely at the King's feet.

During the proceedings conducted by the Commission the Princess had, most unfairly, been given no opportunity of giving evidence on her own behalf, and it was only after the report had been submitted to the King that she first learned of the allegations which had been made against her, when a copy of the report was delivered at Montague House by Lord Erskine's footman. Next day she wrote a letter to His Majesty.

In it she politely, but with good reason, complained that the Lord's Commissioners made their report without her being given an opportunity to "exculpate herself". She emphatically protested her innocence and stated that the "scandalous stories of Bidgood and Cole" were as false as the evidence of Sir John and Lady Douglas had proved to be. She reminded His Majesty that the whole of the evidence had been given behind her back without her having any opportunity to contradict or explain anything.

In a second letter, which she wrote five days later after taking the advice of Mr. Perceval who first read the evidence and the Commission's report, she made the following requests to the King which, she hoped he would think, were "reasonable and just to grant".

That she should be given copies of the declarations made by Sir John and Lady Douglas. As they were the basis of the whole proceedings of the Commission and as His Majesty had instructed the Lord Chancellor to send her a copy of the report she felt that she was entitled to "the foundation on which it rested".

That she should be informed "how many accusers" she had, and who they were.

That she should be informed of the date or dates on which the declarations were made.

That she should be entitled to receive "that redress which the laws of your Kingdom (administering, under your Majesty's just dispensation, equal protection and justice to every description of your Majesty's subjects) are prepared to afford to those who are so deeply injured as I have been".

These requests were granted and on 2nd September all the relevant papers were in Caroline's hands. Exactly a month later, to the very day, she sent a letter to the King, over 35,000 words in length, containing a masterly analysis of the so-called evidence given before the Commission which could have left no doubt whatsoever in the mind of any unprejudiced person of its complete unreliability. She emphasized to His Majesty the seriousness of the main allegation preferred against her by Lady Douglas, which amounted to nothing less than an imputation of high treason. With regard to that charge, she wrote, the extravagance of her accuser's malice defeated its own ends, for the Commission completely cleared her of it and specifically stated that Lady Douglas's evidence was not entitled to any credibility whatsoever.

The Princess also protested, with good reason it may be thought, that, having so emphatically cleared her of the allegation that she had given birth to an illegitimate child, the Commission should have listened to what really amounted to little more than malicious gossip and left it to "His Majesty's wisdom" to decide what conclusions should be drawn from it. What the Princess objected to more than anything else, and she made it abundantly clear in this letter, was not the principal charge that was made against her, because the Commission found that it was not supported by any evidence, but what were described in the report as "instances of great impropriety and indecency of behaviour which must occasion the most unfavourable interpretation." "From this opinion," Caroline wrote, "I can have no appeal. For as they constitute no legal crimes they cannot be the subject of any legal trial. I can call for no trial. I can, therefore, have no appeal. I can look for no acquittal. Yet this opinion on this judgement from which I can have no appeal has been pronounced against me upon mere *ex parte* investigation."

The Princess then proceeded to deal with the evidence of Bidgood and Cole in great detail and asked "if there ever could exist a case in which the credit of the witness ought to have been more severely sifted and tried." As she pointed out, they had both lived with the Prince of Wales before he married and were appointed by him to serve with the Princess after the separation. It was surely not beyond the bounds of possibility that these two servants did not consider that they owed the Princess that undivided loyalty which servants of her own choice might have done. There was every reason to believe that they were appointed to the Princess's household for the purpose of spying on her. The Prince was certainly not above doing this.

Had she not, the Princess asked His Majesty, not as Princess of Wales but as an accused person, a right to be thought and presumed innocent until she was proved guilty? In the happier days of her life, she wrote, before her spirit had been lowered by her misfortunes, she would have met such a charge with the contempt which it deserved. She would have defied her enemies to the utmost and have scorned to answer any accusation except a legal charge before a competent tribunal. Nevertheless she now confidently appealed to His Majesty's sense of justice and hoped to be restored to the blessing of his gracious presence. She trusted that he would confirm to her by his own gracious words his "satisfactory conviction of her innocence".

It is difficult to find words strong enough to criticize the members of the Royal Commission for not having reported at once to the King, after they had examined the servants, that the evidence of Lady Douglas was completely unreliable, and the fact that had they done so it would have greatly displeased the Prince of Wales cannot excuse them. Lord Thurlow, whose advice the King took before deciding to appoint a Commission, had warned him that the charges could never be substantiated. It must have been most distasteful to Lord Erskine, who was an upright man, to preside over the Commission, but the only way in which he could have avoided so doing was by resigning. He had only quite recently succeeded Lord Eldon on the Woolsack and he was, moreover, a friend of the Prince of Wales. Nevertheless, it serves

to illustrate the difficulty in which a Lord Chancellor may sometimes find himself, being, at one and the same time, head of the
Judiciary and a member of the Cabinet.

Having conclusively acquitted the Princess of the allegations
made by Lady Douglas it was not in the best tradition of British
justice to say that the slanderous suggestions of Bidgood and Cole
regarding Sir Sidney Smith and Captain Manby "must be credited
until they shall receive some decisive contradiction and if true are
justly entitled to the most serious consideration." The Commissioners knew perfectly well that the only way in which these
statements could have been satisfactorily contradicted would have
been by allowing the Princess to be represented before the Commission, in which event her counsel could have cross-examined
the witnesses and she could then have given evidence on her own
behalf.

Having regard to the justifiable grounds for complaint which
the Princess submitted in her letter to the King it was not un-
reasonable that she should expect to receive a quick reply. Nine
weeks having passed without even a word of acknowledgement
she wrote again to the King expressing her surprise at his silence.
"Nine weeks of daily expectation and suspense have now passed,"
she wrote, "and they have brought me nothing but disappointment. I have remained in total ignorance of what has been done,
what is doing or what is intended upon this subject." The complete
silence was not only torturing her by the suspense, she continued,
but her character was sinking in the opinion of the public, who
were aware that a report had been made to His Majesty, which
though it acquitted her of committing any crime nevertheless
made grave imputations against her honour. It was also public
knowledge that a copy of the report had been sent to her, that she
had endeavoured to answer it and that she was still, after nine
weeks, in receipt of no reply. The world, therefore, in total
ignorance of the real state of the facts, would soon begin to infer

her guilt. The Princess also stated that she understood that a copy of her reply to the allegations had been sent to the Commissioners and she implored His Majesty to urge them to advise him upon it without further delay.

Six weeks later she received a message from His Majesty through the Lord Chancellor. It is more than probable that the King would have liked to dismiss the whole affair as having been a storm in a tea cup but he appears to have felt that had he done so it might have left his profligate son open to still more criticism and the Prince of Wales was, after all, heir to the throne. In his reply to the Princess's long and fervent appeal, while stating unequivocally that the allegations about her pregnancy had been proved to be without foundation, the King stated that there had appeared circumstances of conduct which he never could regard but with serious concern. "The elevated rank which the Princess holds in this country," he wrote, "and the relation in which she stands to His Majesty and the royal family must always deeply involve both the interests of the State, and the personal feelings of the King, in the propriety and correctness of her conduct." He went on to express his desire and expectation that "such conduct might in future be observed by the Princess as would fully justify the marks of paternal regard and affection which the King always wishes to show every part of his royal family."

But what pleased Caroline more than anything else was the paragraph in which the King stated that it would no longer be necessary for him to "decline receiving her into his royal presence." She replied immediately and suggested that she should come and visit him on the following Monday. No such meeting took place and ten days later the Princess received a great shock when a letter arrived from the King stating that the Prince of Wales, after receiving all the documents relative to the Delicate Investigation, which had been sent to him at the King's request, had informed his father that he intended to consult his lawyers and asked him not to meet the Princess until the Prince had decided what other action to take.

The Princess was justifiably annoyed and immediately wrote another letter to the King which was followed a few days later by a lengthy document pointing out once again how shockingly she had been treated and expressing the hope that her just requests be granted without further delay otherwise she would have no alternative but to disclose to the world, however painful it might be, and regardless of the consequences, "the circumstances of that injustice and those unmerited sufferings which these proceedings and the manner in which they have been conducted have brought upon me."

Meanwhile Mr. Perceval and Lord Eldon, the former Lord Chancellor, had taken up the cudgels on poor Caroline's behalf and made arrangements for what subsequently became known as "The Book" to be printed privately. "The Book" was to be a full and detailed account of the Delicate Investigation and was to include all the depositions and the arguments in the Princess's defence. Although Perceval and Eldon were Caroline's friends their motives were not entirely altruistic for they both hoped that one of the results of its publication would be the fall of the present Government.

When they heard of the King's sudden change of plans they took steps to expedite publication, and after waiting three weeks for a reply to be sent by the King to Caroline's latest letter she wrote on the 5th March 1807 warning His Majesty that the publication of "The Book" would not be withheld beyond Monday next. For the consequences which might follow its publication, unpleasant and hurtful though they might be to her own feelings, she would be content to take all responsibility; but she was convinced that they could not be more unpleasant than if she were to remain silent. As regards any consequences which might well be unpleasant to the feelings and interests of others her conscience would be clear. She felt that she had been extremely patient and had not acted precipitately and had done everything in her power to avoid taking this painful step, but she was not prepared any longer to leave her character or her reputation to the tender mercies of others. A copy of this letter was sent by the Princess to the Lord Chancellor so that both the King and his Government were left in no doubt as to what might happen.

Had "The Book" been published it is impossible to say what the results would have been, but it is not improbable that the persecution of the Princess by the Prince and his friends would have been finally circumvented and the disgraceful episode of the Bill of Pains and Penalties would never have taken place.

The whole situation was changed, however, by the fall of the Ministry of All The Talents when a bill for Catholic emancipation was introduced in the House of Commons. The Duke of Portland then became First Lord of the Treasury, Spencer Perceval was made Chancellor of the Exchequer and Lord Eldon returned to the Woolsack. Caroline's friends were now in power and the Whigs never held office again during George III's lifetime.

So after all "The Book" was never published, except in a limited private edition, because there was no need for it, and the King once more received his daughter-in-law at Court and often visited her at Montague House. This led to frequent protests by the Prince but all his remonstrances on the subject were in vain.

After coming to power the Princess's friends in the new Government, to their great credit, did not forget her and leave matters where they stood, as they might well have done, and on 22nd April a Minute of Council was signed by the Lord Chancellor, the Lord President of the Council (Lord Camden), the Lord Privy Seal (Lord Westmoreland) and seven others, including George Canning who had been a friend of Caroline for some years.

It stated that after the most deliberate consideration of the evidence which had been brought before the Commissioners and of the previous examinations, as well as the answers and observations which had been submitted by the Princess to the King, the Council felt it necessary to declare their decided concurrence in the clear and unanimous opinion of the Commissioners . . . that the two main charges alleged against Her Royal Highness the Princess of Wales of pregnancy and delivery had been completely disproved. The Council further submitted to His Majesty their unanimous opinion that all other particulars of conduct to which the character of criminality could be ascribed had also been satisfactorily contradicted, or rested upon evidence of such a nature, and which was given under such circumstances, as to render it in the Council's judgement undeserving of credit. The Council also informed the King that in their opinion there was no longer any necessity for him to decline receiving the Princess into the royal presence and that she should be admitted with as little delay as possible and received in a manner due to her rank and station. The Council even went a step further and suggested that Caroline should be allotted some apartments in one of the royal palaces.

The Princess's triumph was, therefore, complete and the announcement, soon made, that she was to be given apartments in Kensington was received with general acclamation. The public were entirely on her side and all her troubles might well have been over had the King's mental condition not taken a turn for the worse after the death of his youngest daughter the Princess Amelia in 1810.

This so affected him that a bill was introduced in the House of Commons by Perceval, who was now First Lord of the Treasury, proposing that the Prince of Wales should become Prince Regent. The Regency Act was finally passed on 5th February 1811 but the Regent's powers were limited for twelve months in case the King should recover and be able to resume government of the country. The King, however, showed no signs of recovering, and on 18th

February 1812 the restrictions on the Regency came to an end.

In May, however, Caroline's friend, Mr. Perceval, was shot in the lobby of the House of Commons by a man named Bellingham. The latter had formerly been a Liverpool merchant whose principal trade was with Russia, in which country he had been imprisoned for debt. He had appealed to the British Ambassador for assistance but nothing could be done for him as it had been ascertained that he had been lawfully convicted under Russian law. He refused, however, to recognize the legality of his trial and brooded over his imaginary grievance so long that it eventually affected his mind. One afternoon he obtained entrance to the House of Commons and shot the Prime Minister through the heart as he was walking through one of the lobbies. And so, unfortunately for Princess Caroline, Perceval was no longer alive to take her side when further trouble overtook her later.

On 4th October 1812 Caroline went to Windsor to see her daughter. When she arrived at Augusta Lodge, where her daughter was living, the Princess of Wales was denied admittance. She immediately asked to see the Queen which she did but without satisfaction. She was extremely annoyed at her treatment and wrote an indignant letter to her husband.

It was with great reluctance, she wrote, that she found it necessary to interrupt "the more weighty occupations" of the Prince Regent or cause him any uneasiness on a private matter, but it concerned not only her alone but her daughter, who would one day be Queen of England. She felt, however, that the restrictions which only allowed her to see her daughter once a week could only be interpreted as a slur on her own reputation. "There is a point beyond which a guiltless woman cannot with safety carry her forbearance. If her honour is invaded the defence of her reputation is no longer a matter of choice and it signifies not whether the attack is made openly, manfully and directly, or by secret insinuation and by holding such conduct towards her as

Caroline of Brunswick, the unhappy queen

George IV as Prince Regent

"When George IV from earth descended
Thank God the Reign of Georges ended"
—*Landor*

countenances all the suspicions that malice can suggest." She asked the Prince to remove these restrictions and to give her the opportunity of visiting her daughter more frequently.

It was more than a month before Caroline received any acknowledgement of this letter and it was extremely curt and unsatisfactory. She was merely informed that her letter had been read to His Royal Highness who "was not pleased to signify any command upon it."

The Princess was now determined to carry the war into the open and sent a copy of the letter to the *Morning Chronicle* which published the full text. The Prince Regent's reply to this was to suspend for the time being all communication between his daughter and her mother. Before doing so, however, he took the precaution of obtaining the support of the Privy Council to such action and this was conveyed to the Prince in a report signed by twenty-one Privy Councillors who stated that they were of the opinion that under the circumstances "the intercourse between Her Royal Highness the Princess of Wales and her Royal Highness the Princess Charlotte should continue to be subject to regulation and restraint."

That Lord Ellenborough was one of the signatories need occasion no surprise for he was one of the Lords Commissioners who conducted the Delicate Investigation. That Lord Eldon also signed it requires some explanation. What reason had he to change his mind since he put his name to a Minute of the Privy Council in 1807 which not only completely cleared Caroline of the allegations made by Lady Douglas but stated that the rest of the evidence given at the Delicate Investigation was of such a nature as to render it undeserving of credit?

Such a complete volte-face on the part of Eldon can only be attributed to political expediency. In 1807 George III was King not only in name but in fact. By 1813, however, he was *non compos mentis* and his son was Prince Regent. Lord Eldon's eye was, doubtless, looking to the future, and it is not without interest to remember that on the death of George III in January 1820 Eldon handed over the seals to George IV but they were immediately returned to him. Political opportunism, like virtue, sometimes has its own reward. Later when the Bill of Pains and Penalties was introduced in the House of Lords and Queen Caroline appeared at the Bar of the House to answer grave charges Eldon, as Lord Chancellor, presided over the proceedings of the House, but, to give him his due, he carried out this duty with dignity and impartiality, and it has never been suggested, even by his most consistent critics, that he enjoyed the task.

The Princess of Wales, however, refused to be daunted by this latest rebuff and decided to bring the whole matter to the notice of the House of Commons. By this time she had given up her apartments in Kensington Palace and had returned to Montague House, and it was from this address that she wrote her letter to the Speaker.

On 2nd March 1813 the Speaker rose in the House of Commons and stated that he had received a letter from the Princess of Wales which he proposed, with the permission of the house, to read.

In it the Princess informed Mr. Speaker that she had received from Lord Sidmouth a copy of a report made to the Prince Regent by certain members of the Privy Council to whom, it appeared, his Royal Highness had been advised to refer for their consideration certain evidence respecting her character and conduct. This report was of such a nature that the Princess felt certain that no one could read it without considering that it cast most unjust aspersions against her and she thought it would be wrong of her "to acquiesce for a moment in any imputation affecting her honour."

She went on to say that she had no means of knowing upon what evidence the members of the Privy Council based their report, nor had she ever had any opportunity to be heard in her own defence. She felt compelled, therefore, to throw herself upon the House and upon the justice of Parliament and to require that the fullest investigation be instituted into the whole of her conduct during her residence in this country. She had nothing to fear from any such inquiry, however searching it might be, provided that she was tried by impartial judges and "in a fair and open manner such as the law of the land required." Her only desire was that she should either be declared innocent or proved guilty.

After the debate which followed, although nearly all the speakers reaffirmed the complete innocence of Caroline, no positive action was taken.

All this, however, made no difference to the Prince Regent's attitude towards the access he allowed Caroline to their daughter and he still persisted in his refusal to allow them to meet under any circumstances except with his permission.

He never left a stone unturned to poison his daughter's mind about her mother, as is well illustrated by a letter which he wrote on 16th May 1813 in reply to one from Charlotte asking whether she might be given permission to visit her mother on the occasion of Caroline's birthday.

"I cannot express to you," he wrote, "how much delighted I am with your most kind and affectionate letter. I shall not object to your visiting your mother on her birthday but I confide so much in your own discretion and sense of propriety and what you must feel in the delicacy of both our situations at the present moment that you will see how desirable it is to make this merely a morning visit and not to extend it to that hour of the day when you might be subjected to Society which I might not approve of and which consequently I have every reason to rest satisfied that you would not wish to meet . . . ."

What Charlotte thought of this hypocritical warning and advice from her worthless father, whose only interest in his daughter was to insult and injure his wife, we do not know, but she cannot have been totally unaware of his real character: a man whose friends were dissolute and whose morals were unspeakable, a man who was not unjustly described by Justin McCarthy in these words, "the malignant enemy of his unhappy father, the treacherous lover, the perjured friend, a heartless fop, a soulless sot, the most ungentlemanly First Gentleman in Europe whose memory baffles the efforts of the sycophant and paralyses the anger of the satirist." A man about whom Praed wrote the following epitaph:

> A noble nasty course he ran,
> Superbly filthy and fastidious,
> He was the world's first gentleman
> And made the appellation hideous.

What his father really thought of the Prince, although in public for the sake of the rest of the family he did his best to gloss over his son's behaviour, can be seen from a letter which he wrote shortly before the Prince left Caroline to return to Mrs. Fitzherbert:

The professions you have lately made in your letters of your particular regard to me are so contradictory to your actions that I cannot suffer myself to be imposed upon them. You know very well you did not give the least intimation to me or to the Queen that the Princess was with child till within a month of the birth of the young Princess. You removed the Princess twice, in the week immediately preceding the day of her delivery, from the place of my residence, in expectation (as you voluntarily declared) of her labour; and both times, upon your return, you industriously concealed from the knowledge of me and the Queen every circumstance relating to this important affair, and you at last, without giving notice to me or to the Queen, precipitately hurried the Princess from Hampton Court in a condition not to be named. After having thus, in execution of your own determined measures, exposed both the Princess and her child to the greatest perils, you now plead surprise and tenderness for the Princess as the only motives that occasioned these repeated indignities to me and to the Queen your mother.

This extravagant and ungrateful behaviour in so essential a point as the birth of an heir to my crown, is such evidence of your premeditated defiance of me, and such contempt of my authority, and of the natural right belonging to your parents, as cannot be excused by the pretended innocence of your intentions, nor palliated or disguised by specious words only; but the whole tenour of your conduct for a considerable time has been so entirely void of all real duty to me, that I have long had reason to be highly offended with you, and until you withdraw your regard and confidence from those by whose instigation and advice you are aided and encouraged in your unwarrantable behaviour to me and to the Queen, and until your return to your duty, you shall not reside in my palace which I will not suffer to be made the resort of them who, under the appearance of an attachment to you, foment the division which you have made in my family and thereby weakened the common interest of the whole.

In this situation I will receive no reply; but, when your actions manifest a just sense of your duty and submission, that may induce me to pardon what at present I most justly resent. In the mean time it is my pleasure that you leave St. James's with all your family when it can be done without prejudice or inconvenience to the Princess and the care of my granddaughter, until a proper time calls upon me to consider of her education.

G.R.

In addition to preventing Caroline from seeing her daughter and from attending Court receptions the Regent did his best to prevent any distinguished foreigners who visited London from seeing his wife. She was now living at Connaught House, on the north side of Hyde Park, having been evicted by the Prince from her apartments in Kensington Palace on the excuse that he needed them for another purpose. Even some of her close relatives were tactfully persuaded not to call on her.

This petty persecution was resented by nearly everyone, and the Princess's popularity increased at the expense of the Prince who was hissed and booed wherever he went.

The treatment of the Princess has excited almost universal disgust and I am told she was last night received at Covent Garden with unusual applause and "three cheers for an injured woman". The Regent is getting very unpopular again. He passed us yesterday in a very hasty style in the park, going in state with the Life Guards galloping after him, but not a symptom of applause.[1]

It is shameful [Lady Charlotte Bury wrote in her diary] how our Regent is kicking the dust in the poor Princess of Wales's face. There are moments when her wrongs make all her errors forgotten. There is that little vile Prince of Würtemberg, her own nephew, who has never been to see her. White's Club is to give a great ball and fête, and they have given tickets to the Regent that he may invite the royal family and this on purpose to avoid asking the Princess. Was there anything so shameful?

A few days later Lady Charlotte accompanied the Princess to the opera and on her arrival everyone in the pit and stalls turned to the Princess's box and applauded her.

We entreated her to rise and make a curtsey [Lady Charlotte wrote], but she sat immovable and at last, turning around she said to Lady —— "my dear, Punch's wife is nobody when Punch is present". We all laughed but still thought her wrong not to acknowledge the compliment paid to her but she was right, as the sequel proved. "I know my business better than to take the morsel out of my husband's mouth, I am not to seem to know that the applause is for me till they call my name." The Prince seemed to verify her words for he got up and bowed to the audience. . . . In fact the Prince took the applause to himself and his friends—or rather his toadies—for they do not deserve the name of friends, to save him from the imputation of this ridiculous vanity, chose to say that he did the most beautiful and elegant thing and bowed to his wife! When the opera was finished the Prince and his supporters were applauded but not enthusiastically, and scarcely had H.H. left the box, when the

[1] *The Jerningham Letters*, edited by Egerton Castle, 1869.

people called for the Princess and gave her a very warm applause. She then went forward, made three curtseys and hastily withdrew.

On the way home there were demonstrations of the people's goodwill and sympathy for Caroline. When her carriage was passing Carlton House the mob surrounded it and having found out that the Princess was in it they cheered her most enthusiastically. Some of the bystanders opened the carriage doors, insisted on shaking hands with her and asked if they should burn Carlton House. "No my good people," she said, "be quiet—let me pass and go home to your beds." They would not go away and followed the carriage for some distance shouting, "Long live the Princess of Wales, long live the innocent."

It was not only from the ordinary people that the Princess received sympathy and encouragement at this time. The Lord Mayor, Alderman and Livery of the City of London voted an address to H.R.H. the Princess of Wales in which they expressed indignation and abhorrence at "the foul and detestable conspiracy which by purged and suborned traducers, had been carried on against the Princess's honour and life".

Many meetings were held in the principal cities and large towns in the provinces expressing horror at the nefarious treatment of Her Royal Highness and wishing her happiness "at her complete triumph over her enemies".

These widespread demonstrations of public sympathy and goodwill were, doubtless, of great comfort to Caroline, and she must have regarded them as a triumph of truth and justice and a complete vindication of her reputation. As far as the Prince Regent was concerned, the only effect it had was to make him more determined than ever to continue the persecution of his wife. It was clear to Caroline herself that he would never let her live in peace and would not hesitate to use his daughter as a pawn in the game.

This realization, and events which happened during the year 1814, finally led to Caroline's decision to go abroad, contrary to the advice of Henry Brougham, whom the Princess had been in the habit of consulting from time to time since the end of 1810 with regard to her difficulties with the Prince and particularly in respect of her daughter Charlotte. Although, on occasions, Brougham gave Caroline sound advice and his conduct of her defence during the second reading of the Bill of Pains and Penalties in the House of Lords was masterly, there is an abundance of evidence that he was playing a double game. The account given in his own autobiography is hardly borne out by the correspondence on the same subject published in the Creevey Papers which clearly shows that the politicians were determined "to keep the game alive" and to exploit the unhappiness of mother and daughter to their party's advantage.

The first occasion on which Caroline had consulted Brougham was on behalf of her daughter and at her request. Charlotte wished to know where she stood *vis-à-vis* her father; was she entirely subject to his pleasure and control? It was important for her to know this as she was anxious to have her own home and establishment when, in a few years' time, she would be eighteen years of age. Brougham informed Caroline that the Crown had absolute power over all members of the royal family and, particularly, the reigning Sovereign had the exclusive right to direct their education, residence, and guardianship while under age.

During the whole of 1813 the battle over Charlotte went on, and Caroline wrote letters to the Regent and to the Queen her mother-in-law, some of them against the advice of Brougham. None of them made the situation any easier. Charlotte herself, although she was fond of her mother, naturally had no desire, for obvious reasons, to widen the breach between herself and her father, and she was anxious that nothing should be done by her mother which might have that effect. Hearing that Caroline was intending to write yet again to the Prince, Charlotte wrote to Brougham expressing her apprehension. On this occasion, although he had not always felt happy about some of the former letters, he did not think that it would raise any new difficulties in respect of Caroline's access to her daughter. It was in fact quite harmless and contained nothing more than a polite request to be allowed to see Charlotte once a fortnight. He wrote, therefore, direct to Caroline to that effect.

He also took the opportunity, however, to impress upon her the fact that nothing should be done to give her enemies the slightest pretext for throwing the blame on her, and everything should be avoided which could be construed by the Prince Regent's advisers as a disregard of his authority, however painful it might be. In any event it would not be for ever, as in about four years' time Charlotte would be of age and would then become her own mistress.

But there was another matter of even greater importance upon which Princess Charlotte was shortly to ask Brougham's advice, namely her father's wish to have her married. She was convinced, when it was suggested that she should become engaged to a drunken nit-wit, the Prince of Orange, and there can be no doubt that she was right, that the whole object of the plan was that she should live abroad after her marriage and cease to be a political issue.

Her father was bent upon a match and this formed the subject of a lengthy correspondence between Charlotte and Brougham, through her mother, as to what could be done to prevent it happening.

Caroline was also dead against such a marriage taking place, which is not surprising in view of her own experience, but she did nothing to influence her daughter, although she fully supported Charlotte's attitude.

Charlotte was, however, eventually persuaded to become engaged, but she continued to insist that there must be a proviso in the marriage treaty that she should have the right to revisit England "at her own pleasure".

During the summer of 1814, however, the Prince of Orange came over to England to finalize the preliminary arrangements before the marriage could take place, and he soon discovered that all was not well. Lady Charlotte Lindsay, who throughout the negotiations between Princess Charlotte and her father had been the channel through which the Prince's wishes had been conveyed to Brougham, wrote him an urgent letter in July informing him of the latest developments. She had just returned from Warwick House where Charlotte was then living. "The Princess," she wrote, "had been very anxious to see me having become very suspicious that as no arrangements had so far been made for her to have any place of residence in England after her marriage she felt convinced that 'they' intended to play a trick on her and get her out of England once the marriage had taken place." Charlotte had also told Lady Lindsay that she found the Prince of Orange's attitude towards her mother had greatly changed and that he appeared to be on the side of the Regent. Nevertheless, Charlotte was determined to support her mother and felt that they should both remain in England and protect each other.

While this interview was going on in Warwick House the Prince of Orange suddenly arrived, and Charlotte told him then and there that she would not leave England now and would avail herself of the discretionary power which she had been promised would be inserted in her marriage contract.

When Charlotte's ultimatum reached her father's ears he went immediately to Warwick House and told her that she must leave at once and go into residence at Cranbourne Lodge, Windsor, with a new staff of ladies-in-waiting which he had appointed after dismissing her present household. Charlotte received her father's instructions without making a scene and he left for Carlton House delighted with the day's work. He had hardly left the house, however, before Charlotte drove off to Connaught House where she expected to find her mother. On arrival there she was told that the Princess of Wales was at Blackheath.

What happened then has been described by Brougham in the second volume of his autobiography:

> I was in the midst of dinner when a message came to me that I was wanted at Connaught Place. . . . When I got there to my astonishment I found both my hands seized by the Princess Charlotte. . . . I asked by what extraordinary accident I had the honour and pleasure of seeing Her Royal Highness there. She said, "Oh, it is too long to tell you now for I have ordered dinner and I hope it will come up soon." She only added that she had come out of Warwick House alone, and had got into the first hackney coach she could see and had sent to Blackheath for her mother, who arrived sometime after with Lady Charlotte Lindsay. We sat down to dinner and she was in high spirits, seeming to enjoy herself like a bird set loose from its cage.

Brougham, knowing that the Duke of Sussex was dining in the neighbourhood, wrote a note begging him to come along and an hour later he arrived. During dinner several others came to Connaught Place, having been sent there by the Regent, including Lords Eldon and Ellenborough. The Duke of Sussex, not having been sent by the Regent, was allowed to come upstairs but the others were not. "Old Bags" (the name by which Eldon was often called), Charlotte said, "can wait in his carriage".

After dinner Brougham asked Charlotte to tell him exactly what had caused her to leave Warwick House. She told him that she could no longer bear the treatment she met with of changing her Ladies without her consent and of interrupting her intercourse with her mother and she was determined in future to live entirely with Princess Caroline.

Brougham advised her to return immediately to her own home, which upset her very much and she asked him why he refused to stand by her. He said that he was expressing no opinion about her proposed marriage except that she must follow her own inclination entirely but insisted that it was absolutely essential that she should return home and in this her mother, the Duke of Sussex, Miss Mercer (her great friend) and Lady Charlotte Lindsay, for whom she had a great respect and regard, were all agreed. Eventually she consented to go back to Warwick House and the Duke of York, her uncle, who had just arrived, accompanied her home.

Caroline, even before this incident, had already decided to leave England. She could see no end to her husband's senseless persecution and she thought that if she were out of the way it would eventually make it easier for her daughter. Brougham, however, tried hard to persuade her not to go. The advice was, doubtless, good, but it can hardly have been altruistic, for with the Princess away his principal instrument for annoying the Prince Regent would be gone.

George Canning, however, whom she consulted before making the decision, thought it was a wise one and said so. Being himself a Tory it is very probable that he warned her that the Whigs were exploiting her unhappy position for political ends and there was, undoubtedly, some truth in this. There is no reason to suppose that the motives of one of her most constant supporters, Samuel Whitbread, were not genuine. Before she left she wrote and thanked him profusely for all he had done and had tried to do but she said that she had made the decision because it was pitiable to see a child rendered on all occasions a source of dispute between her parents.

Charlotte, on the other hand, thought that her mother's conduct in going abroad at a time when her presence was most needed was "really heartless". Her feelings were understandable but Caroline can surely be forgiven for thinking that with her out of the way the Regent's treatment of his daughter might possibly improve. That it did not, that he shamefully neglected her, is not sufficient reason for blaming her mother, and it is most unlikely that had

Caroline remained in England Charlotte would have been any happier.

As soon as Charlotte heard of her mother's decision to go abroad she asked Brougham to do his utmost to make her change her mind. There was no need for this, for both Brougham and Whitbread were dead against Caroline leaving the country as both regarded the step as being full of danger. Brougham wrote her a letter solemnly warning her of the risks that she ran. He said that as long as she and her daughter remained in England, surrounded by their friends, he would answer for their safety with his head, but it would be quite different if she went, as she intended, to Italy.

As she still seemed quite determined to carry out her plan Brougham decided to make one last attempt to dissuade her and wrote a second letter ten days before she sailed from Lancing. His reason for writing again was that he still hoped that she would listen to his advice and thereby prevent incalculable mischief both to her and her daughter. He reminded her that he had, all along, been strongly against her leaving, but even if she were determined to ignore his advice he implored her not to do anything which might make it appear that she intended to remain abroad for any length of time. There would be no harm in a short tour on the continent of Europe but reports were already being circulated by her enemies that she was intending to take up permanent residence abroad and nothing should be done to encourage such rumours. Brougham assured her once again that as long as she remained in England he would answer for it that no plot could succeed against her, but if she went to live abroad, surrounded by spies, as she would be, ready to invent and swear as they might be instructed, who could say what might happen. Furthermore, the longer she stayed away the less friends she would have.

Brougham seems to have foreseen clearly what might and, in fact, did happen during her absence and, particularly, the damage that would ensue if she were still abroad when the Prince Regent succeeded his father and she became the legal Queen. She would be foolish, Brougham wrote, if she imagined that it would be time enough to return when she saw steps being taken against her. He hoped that what he had presumed to tell her would not cause offence, though he appeared to think that it might, for when he sent a copy of his letter to Lord Grey on the following day he said that it was "a strong dose but necessary" but that "after making her absolutely furious for some time it will do her good".

But Caroline was not offended and Lady Lindsay wrote to Brougham and told him so. "It seems to have struck her very much," Lady Lindsay wrote, "and although it may not make her change her determination of going abroad next Monday it may induce her to hold herself in readiness to return upon any indication of inimical designs from hence. She has written to Canning to desire him to tell Lord Liverpool that if she hears any alarming reports from England her return shall be immediate."

On 9th August she set sail in H.M. Frigate *Jason*. Having arrived at the Stein Hotel in Worthing about 4 p.m., she had then driven with Lady Charlotte Lindsay and William Austin, the boy whose adoption by Caroline in 1806 had created all the scandal that led up to the Delicate Investigation, to Lancing, two miles along the Brighton road, apparently wishing to avoid the large crowd of people who were waiting at Worthing to see her embark. She was not to see England again until almost six years later when she sailed into Dover Harbour on the *Prince Leopold*.

FOUR

The Years of Exile

ᏆᏪᏪᏪᏪᏪᏪᏪᏪᏪᏪᏪᏪᏪᏪᏪᏪᏪᏪᏪᏪᏪᏪ

CAROLINE could not have been more mistaken in imagining that her sojourn abroad would bring her husband's evil machinations to an end. Brougham's prophecy that she would be surrounded by the Regent's spies wherever she went proved to be only too true, and there is reason to believe that she was even being watched from the moment she boarded H.M. Frigate *Jason*. The Duke of Clarence was alleged to have written to *Jason*'s captain suggesting to him that his amorous approaches to Caroline would not be unacceptable to her and would be forgiven by the Prince Regent.

It was the captain alone who would be forgiven, for the Prince would not have condoned adultery on Caroline's part. Brougham had warned her, "Depend upon it, Madam, there are now many persons who are waiting for a chance of divorcing you from the Prince." She, herself, was well aware of the dangers ahead, and any indiscretions on her part during her absence abroad were committed deliberately but they were of such a kind that, while they might annoy the Regent if they came to his ears, they could not give him any ground for divorce.

When told by a friend that everything she did was known at

Carlton House she said, "I know it and, therefore, do I speak and act as you hear and see. The wasp leaves his sting in the wound and so do I. The Regent will hear it, you say: I hope he will, I love to mortify him."

Her first stop was at Brunswick where she spent two months staying with her brother, after which she left for Milan, spending a few days in Switzerland *en route*. In 1815 she decided to go and live in Naples. There, shortly after her arrival, something happened which, when it was reported to the King of Naples, was regarded by him as highly suspicious, and he immediately reported it to the Princess as he was not prepared to have such a distinguished visitor spied upon while she was a guest in his country.

One day in December, while Count Macirone was walking through the city in company with a retired British general, Montague Matthew, they met an Englishman who was unknown to the Count but was later identified as a Mr. Quentin, a brother of the colonel of the 10th Hussars, and who was believed to hold some appointment in the Regent's household. General Matthew was later introduced to Quentin and asked him what he was doing in Naples. Quentin told the general, with apparent embarrassment, that he had been sent there by the Regent to buy some horses.

It was considered highly improbable that an Englishman would come to Naples, of all places, for that purpose, and the presence of Mr. Quentin and the reason he had given for being there were immediately reported to the Princess of Wales, but she refused to regard the incident as in any way suspicious.

Meanwhile, however, Count Macirone had reported the matter to the King, who instructed the Chief of Police to keep an eye on Mr. Quentin's movements and this was done. When it was discovered that Mr. Quentin was not the least interested in the purchase of horses the King told Macirone to inform Caroline that should the presence of Mr. Quentin, "or any other possible agent of her persecutors", occasion her the least umbrage or displeasure

The Countess of Jersey, mistress of George IV

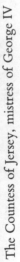

Mrs. Fitzherbert, the morganatic wife of George IV

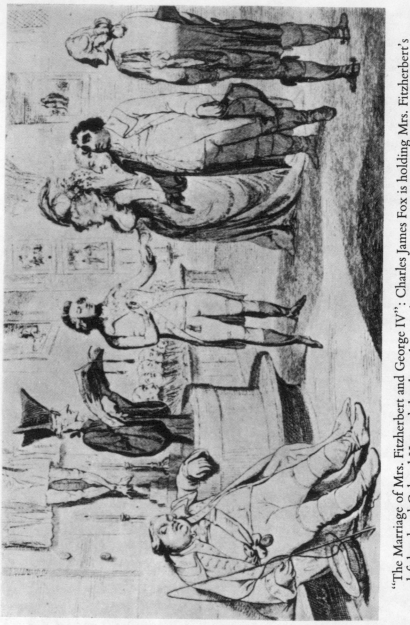

"The Marriage of Mrs. Fitzherbert and George IV": Charles James Fox is holding Mrs. Fitzherbert's left hand and Colonel Hangar's head can be seen between them. Lord North is sitting fast asleep

he would at once take steps to have the offender escorted to the frontier and asked to leave. This message was delivered to Caroline by her physician, Doctor Holland. On receipt of it she informed the King that she was completely indifferent to the activities of any persons who, as she was well aware, might be sent from England to spy upon her, as her conduct was such that "it could never with impunity be misrepresented". Mr. Quentin, shortly after this, left Naples horseless and returned to London.

Count Macirone, during Caroline's stay in Naples, got to know her quite well and was often a guest in her house. "No Princess," he once said, "ever existed who so well combined affability and condescension with the reserve and dignity fitting to her station."

It was while she was living in Milan that she first met Baron Pergami who became the Chamberlain of her household. It was he who was later described in the Bill of Pains and Penalties as Pergami alias Bergami, and throughout Queen Caroline's trial he was always referred to, except by the Italian witnesses, by the latter name, doubtless to convey the impression that he was a dubious character. In fact he came from a highly respectable family but when the Princess met him he had lost all his money. He was one of the Knights of Malta and had served on the staff of Lieutenant-General Count Pino in the campaigns of 1812, 1813 and 1814.

About this time Caroline received some very bad news. Samuel Whitbread, who had regularly corresponded with her since her departure, had died and, on hearing of his death, she said, "I have lost one of my best and most zealous friends."

Meanwhile, she had taken a villa on Lake Como and it was while she was there that the first rumours of her misconduct began to reach London. A Mr. Burrell had been staying with her, one of whose servants was named White. When Burrell and his domestic staff left Lake Como to stay in Brussels, White met some servants of the Duke of Cumberland who were in the Belgian capital on their way to England. The servants started gossiping and White told them wild and untruthful stories about what went on in Caroline's villa. When these stories reached the Prince Regent, as they were bound to do, he arranged for the Hanoverian Minister, Count Munster, to organize a network of spies to watch Caroline's movements. Munster did this and put in charge of it Baron Ompteda, who was then the Hanoverian envoy to the Vatican, and no one better could have been chosen, for Caroline knew his family well and the thought that he could be spying on her never crossed her mind. When she arrived in Rome early in 1815 one of the first people she invited to dine with her was Ompteda and while she remained there he was a constant guest in her house, a snake in the grass if ever there was one. It was not difficult, therefore, for the Baron to obey the instructions which he had been given by Munster, "to locate himself as close as possible to the Princess with the object of accumulating such evidence of her doings as can be brought up against her in court." Ompteda wasted no time and within a fortnight of Caroline's arrival in Rome he was sending back to London scandalous fictitious reports based on material supplied by persons whom he had introduced into the Princess's domestic staff. Pergami was chosen to be the villain of the piece and was described by Ompteda in one of his earliest reports as "a sort of Apollo, of a superb and commanding appearance more than six feet tall: his physical beauty attracts all eyes".

Caroline knew perfectly well by then that she was surrounded by spies. In February 1815 she sent a letter from Naples to Lady Charlotte Bury by the hand of someone who she described in a postscript as "a person who never tells the truth: he is a spy of the Cabal". The letter was written in French. "I have been living here", she continued, "since last November and the place is full of spies. They are a wretched lot."

But there was something which Caroline presumably did not know about Ompteda otherwise she would have suspected his bona fides from the beginning. He had disgraced himself in the eyes of his family and of his country when he accepted the appointment as Ambassador of Jerome Napoleon to the Viennese Court when Jerome became King of Westphalia. Ompteda did all he could to corrupt members of Caroline's domestic staff by means of bribes and other promises, but only one of them yielded to the temptation, a German named Maurice Crede. He undertook to arrange for Ompteda to obtain entrance to the Princess of Wales's apartments by supplying him with a set of false keys, but the plan was discovered and she was informed of it. She took the opportunity of dismissing Crede, giving as an excuse an amorous intrigue which had, apparently, been going on for some time between him and Annette, who was one of Caroline's personal maids.

In the hope of being reinstated, Crede wrote to Chevalier Tommassia who was one of the Princess's gentlemen-in-waiting:

I was yesterday dismissed from the service of Her Royal Highness for having intrigued with her waiting-woman Annette. This event, which has thrown me into the utmost consternation, has awakened in my heart a remorse which had agitated me for some time and which I feel a necessity of imparting to you in the hope that you may interest yourself for me and get me to be received again into her Royal Highness's service.

I must then confess that I merit my disgrace since I suffered myself to be seduced by a certain Baron Ompteda to betray the best of mistresses and the most generous of Princesses. It is about a year ago or about a month before the departure of the Princess that the Baron was to take all possible steps to discover where my mistress slept and to endeavour to precure false keys to her apartment. I persisted for some time in refusing to have any concern in this plot but at length the Baron's threats, who told me I was a ruined man if I did not listen to him, together with the money he offered me from time to time, corrupted me and I was weak enough to accept the commission, although fully persuaded that there was no foundation whatever for the Baron's infamous suspicions.

I must say, however, with the utmost sincerity that the guilt of my conduct went no further than answering the questions put to me by Ompteda in the conferences I had with him in which he interrogated me closely upon the situation of the different apartments in the palace as well as concerning the persons who were about the Princess.

Crede ended his letter with a plea that the Princess should be asked to forgive him.

The letter had been written in Como on 3rd November 1816, and with this definite evidence in her possession Caroline informed the Governor, who immediately took steps to banish Ompteda from the Empire. Lieutenant Hownam, who was Caroline's private secretary, challenged Ompteda to a dual, but it never took place, Ompteda accepted the challenge but left Italy the next day. Nevertheless, he still remained in the pay of the Regent until he died in Rome shortly afterwards.

All these efforts to obtain evidence against the Princess which would give the Regent grounds for divorce, however, produced nothing of any substance. In 1818, therefore, the Prince asked the Lord Chancellor to appoint a Commission to set up an office in Milan and to go through Italy with a fine tooth comb for more satisfactory evidence. The task of setting up the Commission was entrusted to Sir John Leach, an ambitious lawyer who had his eye on the Woolsack. He appointed as investigators Mr. Cooke, K.C., Allan Powell, a solicitor, and Colonel Browne, a former cavalry officer. The Commission cost the tax payer more than £30,000, in those days a considerable amount of money, but it produced virtually nothing of any value.

In any event that is what the Cabinet thought, and the Lord Chancellor was given the unenviable task of informing the Prince Regent when the Commission reported in 1819, of their considered opinion.

Meanwhile Princess Charlotte had died in 1817, after giving

birth to a still-born child. When Caroline heard the tragic news she regretted the distance and the circumstances which had prevented her from seeing her daughter after the marriage to Prince Leopold. She was much criticized at the time for her absence, and perhaps she regretted her decision three years earlier to leave England, although it had only been made because she thought that with her away Charlotte's life would be less unhappy.

During the years of Caroline's sojourn abroad her daughter had remained in close friendship with her mother and it had not been thought advisable by the Prince Regent to renew a quarrel which had proved more injurious to him than to his daughter. It was when she was no longer there to take her mother's part that the Commission had been sent to Milan. Brougham, who during Caroline's absence abroad had been continually in correspondence with some of her friends on whom he felt he could entirely depend, was convinced that after Charlotte's death her mother no longer had any desire to return to England and would be quite happy if some arrangement could be made which would ensure her being free from further trouble and vexation. Her wish, Brougham thought, was to be allowed to assume some royal title in the family and, with an adequate income secured, to be in future officially recognized by the British Ambassador in any country in which she might choose to live.

He therefore wrote a letter to Lord Hutchinson, who was a political as well as a personal friend, and was also on intimate terms with the Prince Regent. The contents of the letter Brougham asked Hutchinson to convey to the Prince. Being certain that Caroline would adopt the plan outlined in his letter Brougham purposely avoided any communication with her so as not to commit her definitely and to make it possible for him to stress that it was only a proposition which he was prepared to put to the Princess and, at the same time, advise her to give it serious consideration.

Caroline the Unhappy Queen

Whether or not, had the proposal been at once accepted by the Regent and his advisers, Caroline would also have accepted it cannot be said with any certainty, but the whole position was shortly to be changed by the King's death in January 1820, when Caroline became Queen and the question of recognizing her position as such became much more difficult than if she had still been the Princess of Wales.

It is only fair to say, and Brougham himself readily admitted it, that the Regent was placed in a position of some embarrassment by certain members of the opposition in Parliament calling for an inquiry into the reports which were circulating about Caroline's conduct and declaring that without such an inquiry they would not feel disposed to vote for the suggested increased allowance for her lifetime.

As soon as the news of the King's death reached her, however, Caroline determined to lose no time in returning home so as to reach London before the coronation and assume her rightful station as Queen.

George IV's first reaction on the death of his father was to ask his Ministers to begin divorce proceedings on his behalf, but Lord Liverpool doubted very much whether there was enough evidence to justify such a course of action and warned the King that the Queen would certainly defend such proceedings and would bring counter charges, *which would be supported by ample evidence* and would bring great discredit not only on His Majesty but on the monarchy itself. He suggested a settlement based on Brougham's proposal to Hutchinson that the Queen should be voted a substantial annuity for life on condition that she lived abroad.

After a great deal of opposition the King saw the red light and, withdrawing his threat to change his Ministers or, alternatively, retire to Hanover, gave way. But it was too late, for the ball was now definitely in the Queen's court and it was most unlikely she would let it go. No one doubted for a moment that Brougham's advice to her would be guided by political or personal considerations, perhaps by both. It would probably bring down the present government if he persuaded the Queen to return and claim her just rights.[1]

For a time Brougham was in two minds what to do but he eventually decided to try and sell the Queen's interest for a silk gown. This was refused by the Lord Chancellor, Lord Eldon, who hated him. Lord Liverpool had asked him to inform the Queen about the offer of an annuity but he did not do so until much later and then he advised her to reject it.

The Queen now decided to go to St. Omer, near Calais, and sent word to Brougham asking him to meet her there.

Meanwhile another of Caroline's most consistent supporters had decided to step into the ring, Alderman Sir Matthew Wood, who had been Lord Mayor of London from 1815–16 and then became a Member of Parliament for the City of London. Like Brougham he was a Whig and had supported Caroline from the beginning of her troubles, but in his case the reasons for so doing were entirely altruistic. He had always believed in her innocence of the charges brought against her and despised her husband for the way in which he had treated her.

He now wrote to Caroline and said that he would come to France and meet her in St. Omer, having heard of her intention to go there from his son who later, as Lord Hatherley, was to become Lord Chancellor in the Gladstone Government of 1868. Young Wood had met Caroline while she was living temporarily in Geneva and had joined her household.

So when Caroline arrived at Villeneuve on her way to St. Omer she found Sir Matthew was already there waiting for her. She at once told him of her determination to return to England, assert her rights as Queen and confront her enemies.

While at Villeneuve she wrote three important letters. The first,

[1] See E. L. Woodward, *op. cit.*

addressed to the Earl of Liverpool, asked that a palace should forthwith be prepared for her reception as she intended to leave for London at the earliest opportunity. The second letter was to Lord Melville, who was First Lord of the Admiralty, asking that a royal yacht be sent to Calais to receive her on board. The third was for the Duke of York repeating the two requests made in the other letters and protesting against the way in which she had been treated. The messenger to whom these letters were handed was instructed to return to France as soon as possible and to join the Queen in St. Omer. When she reached St. Omer the messenger had just arrived with news that Brougham hoped to be with the Queen in two days' time. No replies, however, had yet been received from either Lord Liverpool or Lord Melville.

Two days later, as promised, Brougham arrived at St. Omer with his brother James, and Lord Hutchinson. After the Queen had received them Lord Hutchinson told her that he had a proposition from the King to submit to her. She told him, however, that whatever the proposal was she had no intention of giving any answer to it until after her return home and, in any event, she wished to see it in writing.

This placed Hutchinson in a difficult position and he immediately wrote a letter to Brougham explaining that he did not have any proposition in a specific form of words which he could place before the Queen, but he set out in detail for her information the gist of the conversations which he had had with the Prime Minister before leaving for France. These were in substance the same as he was to tell the Queen next morning when he saw her for the second time. He thought it right, however, to warn Brougham that if Caroline were so ill-advised as to return to England that would mean an end to all negotiation and compromise.

As soon as this letter was handed to Brougham he showed it to the Queen, who was most indignant and asked for his advice.

While admitting that she could not possibly accept the conditions set out in Hutchinson's letter he begged her to consider what conditions would be acceptable. She replied without hesitation, "I shall set out for England. It is in London and London alone that I shall consider any proposals by the King of England."

On the following morning Lord Hutchinson saw the Queen again and repeated the terms of the offer. He also warned her that unless she agreed to those terms and conditions the moment she set foot in Great Britain proceedings would, in all probability, be taken against her.

Caroline listened with mounting indignation and, when Hutchinson had finished speaking, she left the room without saying a word. Shortly afterwards, accompanied by Sir Matthew Wood and her retinue, she left for Calais and about 10.30 p.m. embarked on the packet steamer *Prince Leopold*, her request for a royal yacht having been completely ignored.

Lord Hutchinson was not very pleased with the Queen's reaction to the offer conveyed from her husband and that evening after she had left for Calais he wrote the following letter to Sir Benjamin Bloomfield:

> We arrived here about 3 o'clock yesterday. I saw the Queen for about an hour . . . drank tea with her and left a little after 8. She then appeared calm and collected and I entertained a distant hope that she might be induced to listen to reason. . . . It is impossible for me to print the insolence, the violence and the precipitation of this woman's conduct. . . . I never saw anything so outrageous, so undignified as a Queen or so unamiable as a woman. . . . She has set the King's authority at defiance and it is now time for her to feel his vengeance and his power. Patience, forbearance and moderation have had no effect on her. . . . The Queen has thrown down the gauntlet of defiance. The King must take it up.

Strong words indeed, though it is difficult to understand how, bearing in mind the fact that Lord Hutchinson knew all the past history, he can have been surprised that the Queen appeared out-raged when the King's proposal was put to her. Furthermore, it would have been interesting to ask Lord Hutchinson on what occasion had Caroline's husband ever treated her with "patience, forbearance or moderation!"

In any event it was the King and his Ministers who were trying to bribe Caroline not to return home. There might have been some justification for Hutchinson's unrestrained tirade against her had it been she who was blackmailing the King for an annuity of £50,000 in return for a promise to remain abroad for the rest of her life.

FIVE

The Queen Comes Home

BEFORE the white cliffs hove in sight news reached Dover that the *Prince Leopold*, with the Queen on board, was already on her way across the channel, news which created some confusion, especially among the military authorities, as to how she should be received. After some consideration, but obviously on his own responsibility, as in those days it was not possible to get in touch with the War Office for orders so quickly, the Garrison Commander, Colonel Monroe, decided to welcome Her Majesty with a royal salute. There was really no other decision that he could properly make, for she was, without doubt, the Queen Consort, and his standing orders were to fire a royal salute whenever a royal personage landed at Dover.

His decision was, at any rate, popular with the local inhabitants, who had heard the news of the Queen's impending arrival and were already thronging the quayside to welcome her. The *Prince Leopold* arrived off the harbour just before 1 o'clock, but owing to the tide was unable to enter. The Queen, therefore, decided to come alongside in a small boat in spite of a heavy swell, and as she approached the beach she was greeted with loud cheers from the thousands who were waiting for her.

The following description of what then happened is taken from a newspaper account of her landing which appeared next morning:

At 1 o'clock Her Majesty put her foot on British ground: the royal salute began to fire and a universal shout of congratulation welcomed her arrival. For a few moments her countenance and manner bespoke considerable agitation: she was visibly affected by the cordial symptoms of regard which welcomed her home, but she soon recovered herself and with a firm step, a composed manner, and a smiling but steady countenance walked slowly along the crowded ranks of the principal inhabitants. Well dressed females, young and old, saluted her as she passed with exclamations of "God Bless Her: She has a noble spirit: She must be innocent". The Queen returned the salutations with the warmest marks of affectionate pleasure and repeatedly thanked the ladies for their expressions of cordial attachment. She appeared in good health, her blue eyes shining with particular lustre, but her cheeks had the appearance of a long intimacy with care and anxiety. She is not so much *en bon point* as formerly and her manner and figure altogether seemed perfectly befitting her exalted station. She was dressed with great elegance. As she moved along, the crowd gathered so fast and pressed so closely around her that she was compelled to take refuge in the York Hotel.

Mr. Wright of the Ship Hotel, seeing that it would be impossible for Her Majesty to reach his house on foot, immediately despatched a handsome open carriage to the York. Her Majesty, Lady Hamilton, and Alderman Wood ascended the carriage: the populace removed the horses and drew it themselves. A band of music preceded Her Majesty and two large flags bearing the inscription of "God Save Queen Caroline" were carried by some of the principal tradesmen. A guard of honour was placed at the door of the hotel, but the people did not seem to relish their appearance, and the Queen observing to Alderman Wood that their presence appeared rather to produce an unpleasant and angry feeling, the worthy alderman suggested the propriety of their going away. After playing "God Save the King" the soldiers retired and the populace seemed highly delighted. Her Majesty observed that although she appreciated, as it deserved, the attentions of the commandment, yet she wanted no guard of soldiers: her firm reliance was on the just principles and cordial attachment of her people. Her Majesty then went to the principal window of the hotel and bowed several times with great grace and sweetness of manner to the happy assemblage.

Next day, before she continued her journey to London, a deputation of the inhabitants of Dover asked for an audience so that they could present her with an address of welcome. The request was granted and the address duly presented. In it the people of Dover offered their heartiest congratulations on Her Majesty's safe arrival, expressed "the highest and most profound veneration and respect" for her, and assured her of "their full participation in every happiness which her return might bring to her."

The same evening the Queen left by carriage for Canterbury and was again loudly cheered by the thousands who had come to line the streets and wish her God-speed. By the time she reached Canterbury it was nearly dark but the news of her coming had spread all over the city and on the outskirts she was greeted by a hundred men carrying lighted torches. Here, also, the streets were lined with thousands of people who cheered her all the way shouting: "Long live Queen Caroline."

After staying the night in Canterbury Caroline began the last stage of her journey to London early next morning, Tuesday 6th June, and it was like a triumphal procession all the way. From Canterbury she was escorted by a number of cavalry officers who were stationed there, until she reached Sittingbourne, and in every village through which she passed the same enthusiasm prevailed. All the shops were closed, everyone left their offices, people streamed out of their houses, all to see the cavalcade pass and to cheer their Queen on her way.

It was expected that she would arrive in London some time during the evening and from three o'clock onwards the crowds began to gather. Through Dartford and Greenwich the procession made its way through cheering throngs, many of whom had been waiting since early morning in the pouring rain. As the cavalcade drove down Shooter's Hill the sun came through the clouds, the carriage was thrown open and a roar of welcome greeted Her Majesty. She was obviously delighted with her reception but, as she later told Lady Anne Hamilton who rode in the same carriage together with Alderman Wood, she had expected no less. She had been of the opinion for a long time that the mass of people were sympathetic to her and rightly resented the treatment she had received from the King during the past twenty-three years. As she drove through the streets of London itself she was greeted everywhere with deafening cheers: none were louder than when she passed Carlton House where the sentries on duty presented arms. When, at last, she arrived at Alderman Wood's house she appeared several times on the balcony and bowed her thanks to the jubilant crowd, which immediately dispersed as soon as she disappeared inside for the last time.

What the King's feelings were while all this was going on is not difficult to imagine. Although Greville, in his *Memoirs*, wrote that His Majesty was in excellent spirits and his Ministers affected the greatest unconcern and talked of the time it would take to pass the bills "to settle her business", he added, "Her business, as they called it, will in all probability raise such a tempest as they will find beyond all their powers to appease; and for all His Majesty's unconcern, the day of her arrival in England may be such an anniversary as he will have no cause to celebrate with much rejoicing."

Brougham knew well that no time would be lost after the Queen's arrival before the battle was on again. He managed to return to London before the Queen got there and said to Denman, "now we are for it". And so they were.

On 6th June, the day after the Queen set foot on English soil, Lord Liverpool in the House of Lords and Lord Castlereagh in the

House of Commons laid on the table the famous "Green Bag" containing copies of the depositions made before the Milan Commission together with a recommendation from the King that they should receive the "immediate and serious attention of Parliament".

After reading the King's message to the House of Lords Lord Liverpool proposed that it should be considered on the following day, when he would move that an address be sent by their Lordships to His Majesty pledging themselves to do no more than adopt that course of proceeding which the justice of the case and the honour and dignity of the Crown would appear to require. He would then move that the contents of the "Green Bag" should be referred to a secret Committee "having for its object to inquire whether any and what course of proceeding should be adopted".

When the King's message was brought to the House of Commons, however, an interesting debate took place. Lord Castlereagh, having made a similar statement to that which had been made in the Lords by Lord Liverpool, and the vote of thanks to His Majesty for his gracious message having been carried, Mr. G. Bennet rose and asked whether a letter which had appeared that morning in one of the London newspapers and which purported to have been written by Lord Hutchinson to the Queen's legal adviser was genuine. If so, Mr. Bennet wanted to know whether Lord Hutchinson had received instructions from the Ministers of the Crown to call upon the Queen of England to lay down her right and title—a right held by the same constitutional securities as that of the King himself—for a bribe of £50,000 a year.

Mr. Bennet would not be convinced of the genuineness of that letter until he had heard it admitted by Lord Castlereagh. Until there had been such an admission he could not believe that any British Minister, without the authority and consent of Parliament, could have dared to call upon the Queen to divest herself of her rightful title for such a bribe, not a bribe to be paid by the King himself, but to be taken out of the pockets of the people of England, who were labouring under the severest distresses, and to be given to a person who, if the statements circulated against her were true, was not only unworthy of being the Queen of England, but of being allowed to place her foot upon its shore.

Lord Castlereagh could only get out of this by saying that in the circumstances he did not feel disposed to answer the honourable member's question but that if he wished he could put down a question the following day when an opportunity would occur for its discussion.

This evasive action by Castlereagh only produced further protests from the opposition. Mr. Beaumont thought that the question asked by his honourable friend was very fair and reasonable and he could only assume from the noble lord's decision not to answer it that the letter referred to was genuine and that His Majesty's Ministers were ashamed to own it.

But that was not the end of it by any means. Mr. Bennet was supported by a number of other speakers and, in particular, by Mr. Creevey, who objected most strongly to the action which His Majesty was asking Parliament to take. Had Mr. Bennet not asked the question which Lord Castlereagh had declined to answer he, Mr. Creevey, had intended to move for the production of the papers connected with the recent negotiation at St. Omer. The Queen of England was to be prosecuted for what? For having dared to set her foot in England? His Majesty, Mr. Creevey said, had the same objection to be in the same country with his Queen which he once had to be in the same drawing-room with her. There was now to be a prosecution founded on the result of an unsuccessful menace and an unaccepted bribe, a bribe offered to the Queen of England to renounce her title.

When His Majesty called upon the House to consider the evidence in the "Green Bag" he was, in fact, asking them to become parties in a private prosecution in which the same person was the accuser, a party, the prosecutor, the procurer of evidence, and might eventually, in the event of a Bill of Attainder, be the judge. Since the time of Henry VIII the House of Commons had not been in the habit of interfering with the Queens of England. They should beware before they now ventured on such a course. They should not, said Mr. Creevey, participate with a Cabinet whose fifteen members had on another occasion forsaken their duty to fight against a single woman. Who was she? The daughter of the Duke of Brunswick, the niece of the late King, the cousin and wife of His Majesty and the mother of the lamented Princess Charlotte. Would anyone believe that had Princess Charlotte lived the House would ever have heard of these proceedings? No one would believe it! Mr. Creevey asked the House to pause and think carefully before they put themselves in such a position in which every future step would involve them in greater difficulties.

Before the debate ended and the House adjourned until Wednesday the 7th, when an address thanking His Majesty for his gracious message was moved by Lord Castlereagh, there was a speech by Denman who eventually represented the Queen in the House of Lords during the passage of the Bill of Pains and Penalties. He made it clear at the outset that he had no intention of discussing the King's message, but he felt that before they adjourned Lord Castlereagh should make one thing clear in justice to the Queen, whose arrival in England had brought about the debate. The accusation against her was at present based on documents and not upon witnesses and was to be referred not to the ordinary tribunals of the country but to a secret Committee. He therefore called upon Lord Castlereagh to tell the House when they met next day *distinctly and unequivocally* what was the nature of the proceedings which it was intended to institute against the Queen.

Denman was followed by Brougham who also had no wish or intention to enter into the merits of the case but, he said, unhappily for everybody, for the parties concerned, for Parliament itself, and for the country, a decision appeared to have been taken by the

Government which rendered silence on the subject no longer possible. The time had now arrived when everyone would be called upon to make up their minds upon this most important question. At this moment, however, he would only say this, that in his opinion H.M.G. would not only have to succeed in proving a strong case against the Queen but would also have to convince Parliament and the country that there was no longer any possibility left of postponing or suppressing the discussion of this question. It must be shown that the mere fact of the Queen's landing in this country rendered all further forbearance quite impossible.

It was then agreed upon a motion of Lord Castlereagh that the "Green Bag" should be kept in the custody of the Clerk of the House until the following day when the House would meet again.

So far things had not gone too badly for the Queen. Her return to England and her journey to London had been a triumph, and in the House of Commons the debate had gone strongly in her favour. Lord Hutchinson in a letter to Sir Benjamin Bloomfield admitted that up to the present time the Queen's tactics had been successful and, he wrote, "We have been entirely out-generalled, the violence and the determination of this woman have made her succeed in all her plans."

On Wednesday 7th June both Houses of Parliament sat again to continue the discussion on the King's message. Lord Liverpool immediately moved that a secret Committee should be appointed to examine the papers relating to the conduct of the Queen. The motion was then agreed to and the House adjourned.

Meanwhile, the Queen had not lost any time in addressing a message to the House of Commons answering what the King had asked the House to do. She informed them that what determined her to return to England was the campaign against her honour which had been carried on for so long by secret agents abroad and latterly by the Government at home on the King's instructions. She was determined to have the opportunity of defending her character and maintaining the rights which had devolved on her by the death of the late King.

She was surprised to discover on her arrival that His Majesty had sent a message to parliament asking it to study the contents of the "Green Bag" and she had since learned with still greater astonishment that it was the intention of Parliament to refer these documents to a secret Committee. It was exactly fourteen years to the day since the first charges were brought against her. She had always shown the utmost readinesss to face her accusers and had pressed for a full inquiry into her conduct. All she now wanted was a public investigation at which she could see both the charges and the evidence brought against her, "a privilege not denied to the meanest subjects of the Realm."

She solemnly protested to the Sovereign, to Parliament and to the country, against the formation of a secret tribunal to examine documents which had been privately prepared by her adversaries. This was a procedure unknown to the law of the land and a flagrant violation of all the principles of justice and she relied on the House of Commons to defeat such a proposal.

The Queen's message was read to the House by Mr. Speaker in profound silence, but there were cheers from both sides of the House in support of her demand for a public inquiry.

Lord Castlereagh then moved that the King's message be taken into consideration. The question for the House to consider was what was most likely to satisfy the ends of justice. It would be for the House to decide, after the Committee had reported, whether the case should be brought before the High Court of Parliament or before the Legislature in the form of a bill. He insisted that H.M.G. had been most anxious to avert this painful issue but could do so no longer.

Castlereagh was followed by Brougham, who said that he regretted the whole business as much as the Leader of the House had done. Nevertheless he was glad that the time had come when this question could be fully and fairly met. The Queen, whose cause he was advocating, had not appealed to the mob. Her appeal was confidentially made to Parliament and to the nation and it was now left to him to ask the House to act with justice. He implored them, above all, to believe Her Majesty to be innocent until the contrary was proved.

And what, he asked, was the so-called evidence which was contained in the "Green Bag". Brougham gave his opinion of it and of the means by which it was obtained and he did not mince his words:

> Letters and papers, with or without names, I know not which, forwarded from beyond the Alps, the result of a Commission sent by God knows who. . . . They were the results of a ten months residence in Milan. A man of high rank and learning who stands high in the profession to which I belong and who, till then, was esteemed by all who knew him, procured this evidence. This expectant Master of Chancery had obtained the contents of the Bag.
>
> That individual, who so far lowered himself to engage in such a transaction, went about prying into all corners and mixing in the lowest conversations to pick up idle and malicious gossip. He had mixed with bargemen on the lakes and ferrymen on the rivers and with the company of cellar men and wine servants. He had taken the evidence of cast-off menials. He had gone to the impure source of every pollution and by such means had the Green Bag been filled.

Brougham then asked Lord Castlereagh and his colleagues how they would like to have their conduct similarly examined and made the subject of a Committee. How would they like to be examined in privacy and darkness on documents procured by the same means as the contents of the "Green Bag", and what, he warned them, could wash out the blemish of such a report. How ridiculous it was to liken the Committee to a grand jury, as the Lord Chancellor had done in the House of Lords. The object of setting-up this Committee was to get confirmed the result of a previous inquiry on which Ministers had already expressed their opinion. Let them act on that opinion without going to a Committee. Let them act on their own responsibility without seeking to shelter behind names more respectable than their own. The procedure, Brougham said, was gross, glaring, and unpardonable and after the experience they had had of "Green Bags" and secret Committees they had little reason to be fond of them.

The Queen had commanded him to call for a full, fair, public investigation. The sooner it started and the more thorough it was, the better she would be pleased. She did not care, however, what the inquiry was called, whether it was a grand jury, a secret committee, a select committee, a private tribunal, or even an inquisition. What's in a name? But she did insist that the body called upon to pronounce an opinion on her conduct must give her the opportunity to hear the evidence against her, see the witnesses who gave it, and confront them by every means in her power.

George Canning, who was then still in the Cabinet although he left it six months later, followed Brougham and replied on behalf of the Government to Brougham's indictment. Canning had been a friend of Caroline ever since the days of Montague House and it was partly due to his advice that she had decided in 1814 to go and live abroad. He had not so advised her because he believed in her guilt "but rather to use his own words, 'faction had marked her for its own', and Canning had declared that in similar circumstances he would give the same advice to his nearest relative."[1]

In the opinion of Brougham Canning, in his reply, acted most honourably "and bore such testimony to the virtues and high bearing of the Princess whose honour was assailed by a husband whose whole life and conduct in the marriage statute had been a barefaced violation of his vows," that the Ministers were forced

[1] See *The Life of George Canning*, by Sir Charles Petrie, 1932, page 138.

to give way and an adjournment was agreed to without a division.

It was due to the speech of Mr. Wilberforce, however, that a motion that the House should adjourn until the 9th of June was later carried without a division. He was convinced that there was no member of the House who was not anxious to prevent the investigation proceeding further, if it were possible, for the simple reason that once the step now recommended by H.M.G. was taken there could be no turning back.

The debate was now, therefore, adjourned until the evening of the 9th, but just before it began a communication from the Queen was delivered to the Prime Minister by Mr. Denman, in which she stated that, on the advice of her counsel and several other members of the House of Commons, she thought it proper to inform Lord Liverpool that she was ready to receive any proposition consistent with her honour which he might feel disposed to make on behalf of H.M.G.

She made it clear, however, that she was only taking this step after a great deal of persuasion on the part of her many friends and supporters that it would be in her own interest so to do. Her firm determination, from which she had never wavered, was to challenge her accusers to prove their allegations and to continue to demand the full and unqualified acknowledgement of all her rights as Queen.

Upon receipt of this message just before the debate was to be resumed there was nothing left for Lord Castlereagh to do but to move the further adjournment of the House until Monday the 12th, and this he did. He told the House that he felt it his duty to take this course in consequence of a communication from the Queen which had only just been received by the Prime Minister and the nature of which he did not, at that stage, intend to divulge.

Meanwhile, in the House of Lords a last attempt was being made to avoid taking any action which was certain to lead to trouble in

Parliament and in the country and also to do considerable injury to the monarchy itself.

Lord Liverpool had just moved the Order of the Day calling for the appointment of a secret committee when Lord Kenyon rose to address the House. He wondered whether there might not be, even at this late hour, if not a hope at least a possibility of conciliation, which would avoid the disastrous consequences which would inevitably follow an investigation of the contents of the "Green Bag". He suggested that the House should follow the example set by the Commons and postpone the division until Monday.

This received considerable support but the Prime Minister tried his best to persuade the House to divide without further discussion. He even went so far as to say that nothing had been communicated to him nor had he any information which led him to hold out any prospect of conciliation.

Having regard to the fact that it was to the Prime Minister himself that the Queen had just written to say that she was ready to receive any proposition consistent with her honour, Lord Liverpool was hardly being honest, even by political standards, in failing to disclose the fact that he had received a message from the Queen, although he might have been justified in refusing to give any details as Lord Castlereagh had declined to do in the Commons.

The Prime Minister, was, however, prepared to make one minor concession in order to obtain an immediate division, namely to propose that the Committee should not meet until Tuesday 13th "in order that an opportunity may be given for the possibility of conciliation".

This proposal that the House should proceed at once to appoint the secret committee and then postpone its meeting for one day was hardly a suggestion he can have imagined that the House could take seriously, unless he had a very low opinion of noble lords' intelligence, for, as Lord Carnarvon pointed out, it would have the same effect as the motion which Lord Kenyon was proposing. If the House waited until Monday before dividing, the Committee could still meet on the Tuesday. Nevertheless, the Prime Minister's motion was eventually carried by a large majority.

On the following morning, Saturday 10th June, Brougham and Denman had a consultation with the Queen which lasted for about an hour. Immediately afterwards Brougham received a reply from Lord Liverpool to the message which the Queen had sent to him the previous day. It stated that the Prime Minister had handed a memorandum to Mr. Brougham on 15th April which contained the offer which Lord Liverpool had been instructed by the King to communicate through Brougham to Caroline. Although no reply had yet been received, the letter continued, H. M. Ministers were still prepared to consider any suggestion which the Queen or her advisers might have to offer.

This memorandum had never, in fact, been handed to the Queen, and Lord Hutchinson had gone so far as to tell her in St. Omer that he had no proposals in writing. Nevertheless, the offer made verbally to the Queen by Hutchinson was, to all intents and purposes, the same as that contained in the memorandum, namely that His Majesty was willing to ask Parliament to settle an annuity of £50,000 on the Queen for the term of her natural life, provided she would agree not to set foot *in any part of the King's Dominions* and to assume some other name or title than that of Queen and not exercise any of the rights and privileges appertaining thereto. Should she violate any of these undertakings the annuity would cease forthwith. If she consented to agree to these conditions Brougham was to obtain a signed declaration from her together with full authority for him to conclude a formal agreement on her behalf.

The Prime Minister was informed that the memorandum

referred to in his letter had never previously been shown to the Queen and he wrote next day to express his surprise that this should not have been done.

After an exchange of one or two further useless letters over the week-end a meeting took place between the Duke of Wellington and Lord Castlereagh, representing the King, and Brougham and Denman, on behalf of the Queen, who had suggested that she was willing to leave everything to the decision "of any person or persons of high station and character" agreeable to both the parties concerned with authority to decide the important questions of "residence, patronage and income," subject, of course, to ratification by Parliament.

The Prime Minister's reply to this suggestion was typical of H.M.G.'s attitude to the whole question from the very beginning. After stating that "the King's confidential servants", who ever they might be, could not think it consistent with their constitutional responsibility to advise the King to submit to any arbitration, a matter so deeply connected with the honour and dignity of the Crown, Lord Liverpool went on to say that they were, nevertheless, fully sensible of the advantages which might be derived from a frank personal discussion and were, therefore, prepared to advise the King to appoint two representatives who, in conjunction with a like number to be named by the Queen, could "frame an arrangement to be submitted to His Majesty for settling upon a basis of Lord Liverpool's note of the 11th instant, the necessary particulars of Her Majesty's future situation."

A lot of time and ink would have been saved had this letter never been written. Everybody must have known that it would lead to nothing and was not intended to lead to anything.

During the meetings which took place between the Queen's representatives and the Duke of Wellington and Lord Castlereagh, representing the Government, Brougham and Denman made it clear that the Queen had no insuperable objection to living abroad, and if this were deemed to be indispensable to the completion of an agreement she might be prevailed upon to acquiesce. Nevertheless, in that event, steps would have to be taken to ensure that no inference unfavourable to the Queen's honour and dignity should be drawn from such compliance. One of these steps, Brougham suggested, should be the restoration of her name in the liturgy, to which Castlereagh replied, "You might as well try and move Carlton House!"

The liturgy question put an end to the negotiations and on the following day the House of Commons met in order to be informed of this final breakdown. This was done by Lord Castlereagh, who then moved that the House should adjourn until the 21st so that it could have an opportunity of studying a full report of the negotiations, which would be printed immediately and sent to all M.P.'s

Brougham agreed with what Castlereagh had said about the failure of the negotiations, which he regretted as much as anyone else, but he went on to say that he thought that the whole House would agree, when they had read the report, that there was no reason to blame the Queen for what had happened.

The House having met again on the 21st adjourned once more without doing any business until the next day, when Mr. Wilberforce moved a resolution which was so prolix that he had to explain to the House what it meant, for its real meaning was hidden in a mass of verbiage. The only difference still remaining between the King's representatives and the Queen's legal advisers, he said, were in regard to Her Majesty being publicly acknowledged as the Queen of England in foreign Courts and the restoration of her name in the liturgy. His motion called upon her to waive both these claims and, he asked, would the Queen not go forth without any stigma on her character if she yielded to the wishes and authority of Parliament and after doing so and receiving the gratitude of Parliament would not all imputations against her be removed? He believed that the dignity of the monarchy would always be greater in proportion to the degree in which they conformed to the wishes and feelings of Parliament.

After the motion had been seconded by Mr. Stuart Wortley an important debate took place. Although a large number of members spoke against it, including Brougham, Denman and Sir Francis Burdett, the resolution was carried by a substantial majority.

Dealing with the unfortunate failure of the recent negotiations, Brougham said that the Queen had, nevertheless, gained something, for the only basis on which she had consented to negotiate at all was that she be fully acknowledged in her rank and title. This had now been conceded on behalf of the King. The only other question which admitted of no alternative was an unqualified recognition of her rights and privileges as Queen. The way in which she was now treated and addressed had greatly altered since her arrival in England. Four months ago, Brougham said, there was no possibility of getting the gentlemen opposite even to mention the name of the Queen. They always took evasive action by using such terms as "illustrious personage", "a person of high consideration", "a great lady", or "a lady of great distinction". That was now changed and one heard nothing but "The Queen", "Her Majesty's dignity", "Her Majesty's honour", and "Her Majesty's rights and privileges".

From Calais to Dover she had to sail on an ordinary packet boat and she travelled from Dover to London in a hired carriage. Now she was to have yachts for the channel, and frigates for the Mediterranean and could travel to and fro as she pleased. Those were improvements in her situation but they were not of tremendous importance. The question of restoring her name to the liturgy, however, was *vital* and it did not become less so even if she decided to live abroad, which it was possible she might wish to do. Her leaving England, however, could be misconstrued while charges still remained hanging over her head without being rebutted.

Both Brougham and Denman considered that were her name restored to the liturgy it would prevent any such misconstruction and that is why they had insisted at the negotiations that this should be done. By placing her name in the liturgy every obstacle would be surmounted and it would be easier to restore it than it was to omit it. It had not only been impolitic to remove it but it was also illegal as there was no law in the country which gave the King power to alter the liturgy by an Order in Council. According to the law, in all prayers relating to the Royal family the names had to be changed from time to time to suit the occasion. When one Sovereign died the name of his successor was substituted, and instead of Queen Charlotte the words Queen Caroline should have taken their place.

The specious arguments used by some of those who spoke in support of Mr. Wilberforce's motion that there was no need for the Queen's name to be inserted as she was "prayed for along with other members of the royal family" were not worthy of those who used them. As Denman rightly said, "If Her Majesty was included in any general supplication it was in the prayer for all those that are desolate and oppressed".

More than anything else Brougham disliked the way in which these preliminary discussions in Parliament were dragging on interminably and he hoped that this would be the last time that they would be discussed. It was high time that it came to an end.

Brougham was supported by Denman who reminded the House of the abominable way Her Majesty had been treated almost from the very moment when in 1795 she set foot in this country for the first time. When George III died while she was in Italy she had not even been informed of his death. This was not due to the fact that the Queen was not easily accessible, for the Milan Committee had been there practically on her doorstep and in regular

communication with the Prince Regent and the Cabinet. Her
Majesty had been pre-judged and on no occasion had she ever been
confronted with the witnesses who made the accusations against
her. Not to restore her name in the liturgy would be the final
insult.

Sir Francis Burdett, who also opposed Wilberforce's motion,
was most scathing in his condemnation of the Government's
attitude towards the Queen and left the House in little or no doubt
as to who was behind it all. "He who held a threat in one hand and
a bribe in the other—what was to be thought of him? The threat
was conditional but she rejected the conditions with contempt.
Lord Castlereagh had denied that a bribe had been offered." This
reminded Sir Francis of a character in a play who was asked by a
girl whether taking money was not a bribe, she said, "If you take
money first it is a bribe, but if you take it afterwards it is only
remuneration." His Majesty's Ministers had acted on this principle
but Her Majesty had rejected their remuneration. Then they came
down with their "Green Bag". Mr. Wilberforce had said that this
Bag contained such abominable disclosures of filth that it must
stifle all morality. Sir Francis thought that this was a strange way
of keeping up the dignity of the Crown and he believed that the
Bag was "as false as it was filthy." "This Pandora's box without
hope at the bottom, whether it contained truth or not, should
never be opened. An honest Minister would, if he felt a repugnance
to any act which his master wished him to perform, say candidly
I cannot do it."

At the close of the debate when the Speaker put the question
to the House it was carried by a majority of 267 and the House
appointed the proposer and seconder of the motion, together with
two other members, to "Wait upon Her Majesty and present to
her the resolution of the House".

It soon became known all over London that the deputation of
the House of Commons would present the resolution to Her

Majesty at one o'clock on Saturday, 24th June. Caroline was still staying at Alderman Wood's house in Portman Street and by midday an enormous crowd had assembled. The whole of Portman Street from the Square to Oxford Street was packed with people, nearly all of whom, with hardly an exception, were openly on the Queen's side and anxious to hear what reply she would give. As the deputation arrived at Alderman Wood's house at about 11.5, Wilberforce and Stuart Wortley, who were riding in the first carriage, were greeted with hisses, boos and groans.

Brougham and Denman, who were already with the Queen when the deputation arrived, had decided what attitude they would adopt. They were resolved to give no advice whatsoever and to leave it entirely to her as to whether she would agree or refuse. They both thought it essential that they should take this course because, if she had acted on their advice, it would, in their opinion, have completely destroyed the effect of her determination, and they also felt certain that if they had advised her to comply with the desire of the Commons and leave the country, some of her "violent and secret advisers", as Brougham described them in his autobiography, would have said that although she wished to remain in England and meet the grave charges which were brought against her, her official legal advisers Brougham, Denman, and Lushington were the cause of her going. Brougham doubted very much whether, if they gave such advice and the Queen followed it, they would escape the fury of the multitude. The Queen tried hard to persuade them to advise her but they resolutely declined, saying that the decision was for her to make and not for them: they were merely her legal advisers.

Brougham was most anxious that she should say "Yes" and accept the proposition contained in the Commons's resolution, for that would have saved him from "a most laborious and irksome duty". He also did not want her to have to face the consequences of an inquiry, although he was fairly confident that she had no reason to be apprehensive so far as the result was concerned. What he was afraid of was that she would be persecuted even more than before if she emerged from any inquiry or investigation completely vindicated.

The Queen's advisers withdrew, after the deputation had presented her with the resolution, so that she could come to a decision without them. Later they were called in and told that she would refuse although she would have liked to have their opinion.

When the Queen's refusal was handed to the House of Commons' deputation they expressed their regret and immediately left for Westminster, as the House had decided, for once, to sit on a Saturday so that they could receive Her Majesty's reply.

When the news of her refusal was announced to the waiting crowd outside it was greeted with loud cheers and shouts of approval. As the deputation left the House to enter their carriages there was much booing and hissing and they only narrowly escaped violence.

After the four M.P.s had driven away and Brougham and Denman, who were well received by the crowd, had followed them, there were calls for the Queen, who appeared on the balcony to acknowledge the cheering, which lasted for several minutes.

The text of Caroline's message was as follows:

I am bound to receive with gratitude every attempt on the part of the House of Commons to interpose its high mediation for the purpose of healing those unhappy differences in the royal family which no person has so much reason to deplore as myself. And with perfect truth I can declare that an entire reconcilement of those differences, effected by the authority of Parliament on principles consistent with the honour and dignity of all parties is still the object next to my heart. I cannot refrain from expressing my deep sense of the affectionate language of these resolutions. It shows the House of

Commons to be the faithful representative of that generous people to whom I owe a debt of gratitude that can never be repaid. I am sensible, too, that I expose myself to the risk of displeasing those who may soon be the judges of my conduct. But I trust to their candour and their sense of honour confident that they will enter into the feelings which alone influence my determination. It would ill become me to question the power of Parliament or the mode in which it may be exercised. But however strongly I may feel the necessity of submitting to its authority, the question whether I will make myself a party to any measure proposed must be decided by my own feelings and conscience and by them alone. As a subject of the State I shall bow with deference and, if possible, without murmur to every act of the sovereign authority. But, as an accused, an injured Queen, I owe it to the King, to myself, and to all my fellow subjects, not to consent to the sacrifice of any essential privilege or withdraw my appeal to those principles of public justice which are alike the safeguard of the highest and the humblest individual.

The disappointment of the Government at the Queen's refusal was profound and genuine, unlike the King's, for he was bent only upon some action which would expel his consort from England never to return. All he wanted was his Bill of Pains and Penalties, including a divorce clause. H.M.G., however, and Canning more than any of them, had only one desire—to see the whole business ended once and for all.

The Queen's rejection of the advice of Parliament had definitely closed the door to further negotiations and the Government could no longer delay proceeding with the investigation by the secret committee which the House of Lords had already appointed.

Realizing that there was no time to lose, the Queen's next move was to send a petition to the Lords appealing strongly against the measures to be taken against her and demanding that she be heard by counsel at the Bar of the House.

The petition informed the House that she was perfectly ready,

George Canning

Charles James Fox

The interior of the House of Lords during the trial of Queen Caroline, 1820

as she had always been, to meet every charge affecting her honour and she called for a complete investigation of her conduct, but not a secret inquiry. She could not suppose, however, that the House of Lords would commit such a travesty of justice as to authorize a secret examination of her conduct, in the absence of herself and her counsel, while her defence must rest on evidence abroad which for some weeks could not be available in this country. When such evidence arrived the Queen would ask the House to proceed in any way they might think consistent with the ends of justice. Meanwhile, and before the first step was taken, she desired to be heard by her counsel at the Bar of the House of Lords immediately.

As soon as the petition from her had been read by the Clerk at the table of the House Lord Dacre, who had presented it, moved that counsel should be called in. The question being put by the Lord Chancellor and agreed to without opposition, Mr. Brougham, Mr. Denman and Mr. John Williams appeared at the Bar and Brougham addressed the House on the Queen's behalf and explained his position. The application being made, he told their Lordships, must not be understood to be, in the vulgar sense of the word, an application for delay of the prosecution or of the judgment, but the Queen was entitled to expect and to request that she would receive a fair and equitable investigation at their Lordships' hands. Her Majesty and her counsel had a right to know what proceedings were about to be instituted in both or either of the Houses of Parliament. The Bags laid before both Houses were said to contain evidence to support charges against the Queen's conduct whilst resident abroad. What was not known, however, was the nature of the evidence or how it had been "raked together" except that a great deal of it had been procured beyond the Alps and the Appenines and it would, therefore, be physically impossible to produce the necessary evidence for her Majesty's defence within at least six weeks. The more innocent the Queen was, Brougham said, the more abominable, base and treacherous the witnesses to testify against her were, the more essentially necessary did it become that she should have available those witnesses and documents which she was quite confident she could get to overwhelm her opponents with confusion.

There was another factor, Brougham said, which made her defence more difficult. Practically every one of the witnesses who would be called to support whatever charges might be brought against her were foreigners with whom the obligation of an oath might be diminished by their belief in the efficacy of subsequent confession. Counsel did not hesitate to say that it was his firm belief that not one of their Lordships would fail to tremble with apprehension if his wife or daughter were to be exposed to the testimony of such a cloud of witnesses. Furthermore, Her Majesty was not in a position to compel the attendance of those who could speak in her favour: they could not be subpoenaed. They could refuse to attend and she had no power to force them.

All he asked, Brougham said, was that the House would not proceed to hear the case in a manner which must inevitably lead to the condemnation of any individual however innocent. Her Majesty must be given time to bring forward her witnesses. Brougham was followed by Denman, and the Earl of Liverpool then moved that the petition should be considered next day in order that they might have twenty-four hours to deliberate on the powerful arguments which had been submitted by counsel.

The House met again, therefore, on the Tuesday evening, when Earl Grey made a last effort to stay the proceedings of the secret committee by moving that the order already made for its appointment be discharged. After a long debate, however, his motion was defeated by a majority of fifty-five.

The proceedings of the House of Lords on these two fateful days had been closely followed all over the country and a series of meetings was held throughout the length and breadth of the land for the purpose of presenting addresses of sympathy and support for the Queen. But the die was now cast, and only seven days were to elapse before the Bill of Pains and Penalties was introduced in the House of Lords by the Prime Minister.

SIX

Pains and Penalties

ରେ ୧୬ ରେ ୧୬ ରେ ୧୬ ରେ ୧୬ ରେ ୧୬ ରେ ୧୬ ରେ ୧୬ ରେ ୧୬ ରେ ୧୬ ରେ ୧୬ ରେ ୧୬ ରେ ୧୬ ରେ

ON WEDNESDAY 15th July the House of Lords met, the main business on the Order Paper being the first reading of the bill which was presented to the House by the Prime Minister.

He said that even were it possible for him to retrace the steps he had so far taken he did not know of any other course he could have adopted than that which had finally been decided upon. Although the Bill could not be considered a bill of divorce in the ordinary sense of the word, its effect would be the same. When it had been read to the House by the Reading Clerk a copy would be sent to the King and to the Queen and the first question then to be considered would be whether to fix a date for the second reading immediately or to postpone such decision for two or three days in order to ascertain the wishes of their Majesties.

The whole subject was of the utmost importance, the Prime Minister went on, and called for a dispassionate inquiry. It was satisfactory to reflect that no similar case had arisen during a period of two hundred years, except in the instance of one individual who never came over to this country. There had not been a Queen during that time against whom even a whisper of shame had been raised to affect her character or sully her reputation. The question now was, if the allegations were proved to be true, whether impunity should be extended to guilt or justice be allowed to triumph.

It was most improper of the Prime Minister to say this at that stage of the proceedings unless he was also prepared to say that it was a long time since there had been such a profligate and debauched King as the present one, and that there had, perhaps, never been a King of England more worthless.

The preamble of the Bill which was then read by the clerk was as follows:

BILL TO DEPRIVE HER MAJESTY CAROLINE AMELIA ELIZABETH OF THE TITLE, PREROGATIVE, RIGHTS, PRIVILEGES, AND PRETENSIONS OF QUEEN CONSORT OF THIS REALM, AND TO DISSOLVE THE MARRIAGE BETWEEN HIS MAJESTY AND THE SAID QUEEN.

The Bill alleged that the Queen had conducted herself both in public and in private with indecent and offensive familiarities with Bartolomo Pergami who was engaged in her service and had carried on with him a disgraceful, licentious and adulterous intercourse to the great scandal of the royal family, and that she should, therefore, be wholly deprived of the style and title of Queen Consort and that the marriage between His Majesty and the Queen should be dissolved and annulled.

Lord Grey objected to the way in which the Bill had been drafted. Instead of making general accusations without any specifications of time and place, these should have been clearly stated to enable the Queen to meet the charges. He wished to know whether any more particular details of the offences would be laid before the House and was it intended to supply Her Majesty with a list of the witnesses by whom she was accused?

To this the Prime Minister replied that after the close of the case for the prosecution time would be given to Her Majesty to enable her to rebut the evidence adduced against her.

Next day about noon Sir Thomas Tyrwhitt, who held the office of Black Rod in the House of Lords, and who had been commanded by the House to deliver a copy of the Bill to Her Majesty, waited upon her. She entered the room where he was and received the Bill graciously. "I am sorry that it comes so late," she told him, "for twenty-five years ago it might have been of some use to His Majesty. But as we shall not meet again in this world I hope we shall in the next," and then she paused for a moment, "Where justice will be rendered me."

She then asked Black Rod to convey these sentiments to the King if ever he got the opportunity. Sir Thomas had not seen Caroline since the time when she and the King were still living together and he said, later, that he would never forget what she said to him until his dying day.

He had scarcely left the Queen's presence when a deputation arrived from Westminster headed by Sir Francis Burdett, who had made such a moving speech in the House of Commons during the debate on the Queen's message. The deputation brought with them a loyal address from the citizens of the City of Westminster, for which she was most grateful and handed them a long reply. The address would long be treasured in her memory, it stated, as a lasting proof of their regard. The last occasion on which she had received the sympathy and understanding of the people of Westminster was at the time of the Delicate Investigation, which they truly described as "a nefarious conspiracy against her honour".

The people of England almost universally on that occasion considered the outcome of the investigation as a triumph of rectitude and innocence over perfidy and falsehood. Now new and even more appalling efforts were being made to destroy her character, but she was delighted to find that those same people felt that she was entitled to have her reputation unsullied until she had been proved guilty.

On Monday 17th July the House of Lords met again, when

Lord Liverpool moved that the Bill should be read a second time on 17th August. There was no opposition to this, although Lord Grey said that he thought that the Queen should be given sufficient time to prepare her defence.

Lord Holland told the House that he could think of no reason why the names of the witnesses should not be disclosed and, if possible, copies should be made available of the precise evidence that would be offered. The ends of justice could not properly be met unless the necessary information was given to the Queen's legal advisers and sufficient time allowed for them to examine the evidence.

Even Lord Erskine, the former Lord Chancellor, who had presided over the Committee of the House which had carried out the Delicate Investigation agreed that Her Majesty ought to have the advantage of knowing who the witnesses were so that their character and antecedents could be inquired into. That appeared to him to be essential in the interest of justice. The motion, however, was carried without a division.

The Prime Minister was obviously determined that there should be a maximum attendance when the House was to reassemble on 17th August, for he moved a resolution, which was passed without a division, that no peer should absent himself on that day or any other day during the passage of the Bill without leave of the House, "On pain of incurring a fine of £100 for each day's absence, unless he was over seventy years of age, sick, or had been abroad since the 20th of July and was still away, or was overseas on His Majesty's Service or on account of the death of a parent, wife, or child." The Lord Chancellor was ordered to write to every Peer acquainting him of this resolution. The Government certainly meant business.

Between the day on which the Bill had its first reading and the date fixed for the second reading Caroline received numerous addresses and messages of good will and encouragement from nearly every part of the country. From Poole, Newbury, Shaftesbury, Newcastle, Bedford, City of London, Rochester, Morpeth, Wakefield, Ilchester, Sunderland, Lewes, Berwick, Canterbury, Norwich, Kirkcudbright, most of the London boroughs and one signed by 7,800 women from the town of Nottingham. All of these, without exception, assured Caroline of their sympathy and their thoughts for her during the trying days which lay ahead. The women of Nottingham wrote, "All in whom the spirit of the days of chivalry is not utterly extinct, all who would not immolate the best impulses of their nature on the altar of modern policy will rally around their Queen and save her alike from foreign enemies and spies and domestic persecutors."

On Thursday 17th August the House of Lords in its legislative and quasi-judicial capacity met to resume their proceedings on the Bill of Pains and Penalties, better known as the Trial of Queen Caroline.[1]

At 8.30 a.m. the Lord Chancellor, Lord Eldon, arrived and took his seat on the Woolsack and at 10 a.m. the roll of peers was read and several were excused on various grounds. The three Roman Catholic peers, the Duke of Norfolk, the Earl of Shrewsbury and Lord Petre, were excused on account of their religion. The Duke of Sussex, to his credit, obtained leave of absence because of the ties of consanguinity which existed between him and the parties so intimately connected with the Bill. The Duke of York, his brother, however, said that if anyone had stronger claims than another to ask for leave of absence he was that person, but he did not intend to allow any private feelings to deter him from doing his duty, however painful it might be. He had obviously received the family Whip!

[1] Although the proceedings in the House of Lords were not a trial in any legal sense and no criminal charges were, in fact, preferred against the Queen, in the account of the proceedings which follows they will frequently be referred to, as a matter of convenience, as "the trial".

As the names were being called the shouting of the crowd waiting outside in Palace Yard announced the Queen's arrival. Since the early hours of the morning thousands of people of every kind had been assembling in the streets leading to the Houses of Parliament. Shortly before ten o'clock the sound of cheering from the direction of Charing Cross gave the crowds waiting outside the Houses of Parliament warning of the Queen's approach. Along the whole of the route from her house to Parliament Square she was greeted with tumultuous cheers and they were never louder than when she passed Carlton House, where the sentries on duty spontaneously and, in all probability contrary to orders, presented arms and were loudly cheered by the crowd for the compliment. The sentries outside the Admiralty and the Horse Guards did the same, only the guard outside the Treasury took no notice of her.

At the entrance to the House the Queen was received by Black Rod and Brougham, who escorted her to the waiting-room which had been provided for her. As she entered the Chamber by the passage leading from the robing-room the peers rose to receive her. When she was seated the Earl of Liverpool moved that the Order of the Day for the second reading of the Bill be now read, and the Duke of Leinster, who had previously given notice, moved that the same order be rescinded, but on a division his motion was defeated by 206 votes to forty-one.

When the Prime Minister rose a second time to propose that counsel should be called and heard in support of the Preamble of the Bill there was a lively debate during which the "inexpediency and mischievous nature of the Bill" was argued by a number of peers, one of whom stated that the House of Commons shared this view as they had declared that whatever the result of the proceedings they would be "injurious to the best interests of the Empire."

As many peers expressed a doubt whether, as the alleged

adulterous intercourse had been committed abroad with a foreigner, it exempted the Queen from the consequences of the statute of Edward III relating to high treason, the judges present were asked to decide "whether, if a foreigner owing no allegiance to the Crown violates the wife of a King of England in a foreign country and she consents to such violation, she thereby commits high treason within the meaning and true construction of the statute of Edward III."

The judges retired and returned after an absence of twenty minutes, whereupon the Lord Chief Justice gave the House their unanimous opinion that "such an individual, under such circumstances *does not* commit high treason within the meaning of that Act".

Counsel were then called upon to appear at the Bar and Brougham addressed their lordships and advised them against proceeding any further with the Bill. His first reason for objecting was on the grounds that the Bill was private law introduced in a particular case for the punishment of an individual. It was a mode of procedure known unhappily in the jurisprudence of all countries but never resorted to without producing a deep sense of its hateful consequences and its utter repugnance to every sound principle of jurisprudence and he gave the House several historical illustrations. In this case Her Majesty was gravely prejudiced by this form of procedure. Had impeachment been resorted to in this instance she would have been furnished with some specification of the charges, or at least they would have been set out in greater detail as to the various points of the accusation. Perhaps also a list of witnesses could not then have been withheld and the Queen would have had all the advantages of a real judicial proceeding.

In this case, however, the charge was not any illegal act and the whole proceeding was legislative and not judicial. For this reason Brougham felt bound to discuss the expediency, as well as the justice, of this prosecution. What was the impelling and overruling necessity (he did not say motive for that might be guessed) which alone could justify this measure? The question at issue was not between man and wife but between King and Queen, and the promoters of this Bill delayed until they thought that at least she was deprived of one protection. If she had been brought before the House when Princess of Wales, and charged with offences alleged to have been committed in that capacity, no one could deny that a bill of divorce from her royal husband would have been the remedy and that divorce could only have been obtained on the usual terms. All the preliminary forms would have had to be observed, the party claiming the bill would have had to come to the House by petition, and he would have come in vain if he had not done so *with clean hands*. But here the promoters of this Bill waited until the Queen had lost her status as Princess of Wales and then said "we will proceed against her for offences alleged to have been committed while she was, in fact, Princess of Wales"; thus taking special care not to take any action while she still possessed those rights against her husband which every ordinary wife enjoys.

Counsel then dealt with the question of why it was argued by the Government that the passage of this Bill was a matter of public necessity because the Queen had been guilty of "improper familiarity". She was charged with licentious and adulterous conduct which, the Government stated, made it absolutely necessary for Parliament to intervene. Brougham appealed to the many Bishops present and asked them a direct question. Is adultery considered a crime only when it is committed by a woman? And he then proceeded to ask them another question, whether the Crown could be dishonoured, the fame of the country tarnished and the morals of the nation put in jeopardy if an adulterous intercourse is proved against a lady when that which he (Brougham) ventured to call adultery, because the exalted person himself had confessed it to be so, has actually been committed by a Prince. Counsel said that he regretted having to say this but he was forced to do so because it was, in truth, an answer to this case.

Whatever Parliament might think of it Counsel was sure that the good sense of the nation could not be deceived. "He is a man," the people will say, "who wishes to get rid of his wife. He talks of the honour and safety of the country, yet its dearest interests, its peace, its morals and its happiness are to be sacrificed to gratify his desires." The only way to judge the sincerity of what men professed was to look at their conduct. Who had encouraged the Queen to go abroad? Who had opposed the advice given to her by her friends, including counsel himself, that they would answer with their heads for her safety while in England but that when abroad she would be surrounded by spies and informers? The persons who had encouraged her were those who were now lined up against her, with a Green Bag of documentary evidence in one hand and this bill of degradation in the other, and they had done everything they could to encourage the Queen to stay abroad. She was warned not to come back and, in case that was not enough to deter her from returning home, she was to be bribed to stay away.

As Brougham sardonically put it, she was to be given a large income to enable her to be wicked on a large scale. All levity, all indiscretion, even adulterous intercourse was to be pardoned or condoned on one condition, namely that she would never come back. *Bearing all that in mind how could any sensible man believe that H.M. Ministers in their heart of hearts really supported the Bill?* It would never have seen the light of day if the Queen had turned back from St. Omer after the meeting with Lord Hutchinson, and it was only after she landed at Dover that anyone began to think of "national degradation".

Before he sat down Brougham told their Lordships that the fact that the secret Committee had reported in favour of this action being taken did not bind the House from taking a different view. "He is the greatest of all fools," Brougham said, "who consults his apparent consistency at the expense of his absolute ruin. The sooner you retrace the step into which you may have been led in an unwary moment the greater will be the service you render to your country. If you decide that the Bill ought not to proceed you will be the saviours of the State and, indeed, promote the substantial welfare of the kingdom and the trust and honour of the Crown".

The House then adjourned until the following day, when Denman was also heard in support of the Queen. He ended a powerful speech by telling the House that the Queen had demanded a proper trial with the opportunity of herself denying the charges. The Bill was no alternative and was calculated only to bewilder and betray. The public viewed it with the gravest suspicion.

Before the House adjourned until Saturday the 19th, both the Attorney-General and the Solicitor-General spoke on behalf of the Crown. Theirs was not an easy task and their speeches made little impression on the House. When the Solicitor-General sat down Brougham was given an opportunity of being heard a second time. He maintained, once again, that there were no public grounds for these proceedings. There had been no public inquiry until their Lordships decided to act on the recommendation of the King's Ministers and the whole proceedings had for their foundation nothing but rumour. He said that he did not wish to enter into the realms of recrimination but he felt some relief in knowing that in so doing he had only acted in the discharge of his professional duty.

Lord King then moved a resolution to be debated when the House reassembled on the following day: "That it is the opinion of this House that it is not necessary to the public safety, nor the security of the Government to pass this Bill".

When the House met next day, the third day of the trial, Lord

King's motion and a similar one by Earl Grey, both of which advised the House not to proceed further with the Bill, were defeated by substantial majorities. The Attorney-General then outlined the evidence to be given in support of the charges set out in the Bill.

The Attorney-General said that the adulterous intercourse was alleged to have been committed by the Queen with Pergami, his real name, but which the Attorney-General insisted throughout the entire proceedings was Bergami for reasons which have already been suggested.

Bergami, he told the house, at the time he entered Her Majesty's service was without employment but she appointed him as her courier. Three weeks later the Princess of Wales, as she was then, left Rome and went to live in Naples. With her was the boy whom she had adopted, named William Austin, who, Lady Douglas had told the Committee which conducted the Delicate Investigation, was her own illegitimate child.

Having regard to the fact that the Delicate Investigation Committee had found that there was no truth in Lady Douglas's accusation whatever, it was extremely dishonourable for him to have mentioned the allegation without making it clear to the House that it had been dismissed as a palpable lie in the report which the Delicate Investigation Committee had submitted to George III. The fact that he did so shows to what extent the Government and their legal advisers were prepared to go.

The Attorney-General then told the House that, until the move to Naples, Willikins, as Caroline used to call him, had been in the habit of sleeping in her bedroom. On the first night spent in her new home the same arrangement continued and Bergami was allotted a bedroom at the other end of the house where all the domestic staff had their quarters. Next morning, however, they learned with some surprise that in future Bergami was to sleep in another room, from which there was a communicating passage leading to the Princess's room, and Willikins was, in future, to have a bedroom of his own. She explained that this was because he had now reached an age when it was no longer becoming for him to sleep in her room.

On the following evening the Princess returned home late, having been to the Opera House, and went straight to her room where her maid, Louisa Demont, was waiting for her. Louisa was given strict orders that Austin was not to be admitted to her room that night, and she then saw the Princess go in the direction of the room assigned to Bergami and, as she did so, she told the maid that she could go as she would not be needed any longer. This young woman thought that her mistress's behaviour was rather extraordinary and became highly suspicious, for on entering the Princess's bedroom it was evident that the bed had not been slept in. It was equally apparent that two persons had been sleeping in Bergami's bed.

From then onwards the servants noted a marked change in his attitude to the other members of the staff. He became "more haughty and assumed an air of great importance". They were also struck by the fact that the Princess and Bergami always rose at the same time each morning and had breakfast together in a room which was "completely secluded from the rest of the family", and the Princess was frequently seen walking arm in arm with him on the terrace in front of the house.

Shortly afterwards a servant was engaged to wait on Bergami, and this man, who slept in a room close to that which was occupied by his master, had stated on a number of occasions that he saw the Princess, after the other servants had retired for the night, walking stealthily and with great caution from her own to Bergami's room, which she entered and in which she remained for a considerable time. On one occasion while the Princess was in Bergami's room, his servant heard noises which convinced him that the Princess and "her lover" were kissing each other.

During the whole period during which the Princess was living in Naples, which was from November 1814 to March 1815, this intimacy continued and evidence would be called, the Attorney-General said, to prove it. It would also be proved that at that time Bergami was still a married man and this aggravated the charge now made against Her Majesty. It was not merely adultery but double adultery.

From Milan, the Princess moved to Venice and by this time only one member of her entourage was of English nationality, Mr. Burrell, and after he left, a month later, the Princess became more familiar with all her servants and she frequently played cards with them.

It must have seemed strange that the Attorney-General should mention this and he appears to have realized it for he hastened to add that he was not suggesting that this amounted to an offence but that it was a "circumstance arising out of her infatuated and licentious attachment". This clearly showed how little the Attorney-General really knew about the Queen, who was always extremely sociable and courteous and a very kind and considerate mistress. It also demonstrated, beyond doubt, how slender was the case against the Queen and how the prosecution had to clutch at every straw.

On leaving Venice, the Attorney-General told the House, the Princess returned to Milan and while she was there paid a visit to Mont St. Gothard, and Bergami went with her. *En route* they stopped for lunch at an inn in Vannes where the couple spent the afternoon, according to one witness, in one of the bedrooms. As this happened in the daytime the Attorney-General suggested that there could only be one reason for this.

The following night the Princess's party slept in Borromeo, which she had visited on a previous occasion, when she was, not unnaturally, given the best bedroom that the hotel could offer. It was only reasonable to expect that on her second visit there she

Count Pergami, alias Bergami

Henry Brougham in 1810

Queen Caroline returning from the House of Lords, 1821

would occupy the same room and it was, in fact, the Attorney-General said, offered to her but she did not take it. It did not, however, have any means of communication with any other room and the Princess, on this occasion, chose another much smaller room which happened to have a door adjoining the room in which Bergami spent the night. Their Lordships, the Attorney-General said, would presumably draw their own conclusions from that. Was it not obvious that she took care on that occasion that his room should be near hers for no other reason but to afford the means of carrying on that intercourse which, according to the evidence already mentioned, had been going on for some time? The Attorney-General continued to give many more instances of this kind until the House adjourned, when he said he would finish his opening speech on the following day.

When the House met on the fourth day of the trial the Attorney-General continued his summary of the evidence which he would be calling later. On 8th April 1816, at Salma, an incident happened which the Attorney-General was satisfied would remove from their Lordships' minds any doubts, if any still remained, about the adulterous intercourse between Bergami and his mistress. A large bed was provided in an inner room in the hotel for the Princess, while in an outer adjoining room which was assigned to Bergami there was no bed. It would be proved in evidence that on the morning after she had slept there her bed had the appearance of having been slept in by two persons. The only way into the Princess's bedroom was through Bergami's. In any ordinary case, in a court of law, the Attorney-General said, this would be sufficient proof to a jury that the "crime of adultery" had been committed that night.

For at least another hour more incidents of this kind were submitted by counsel as evidence to support the most serious charge set out in the Bill's preamble, but before he sat down he dealt with the comments by his learned friends (Brougham and

Denman) about the unsatisfactory way in which the evidence had been obtained and the doubtful reputation of the witnesses who had supplied it. It was the fault of Her Majesty if the facts could not be proved except by Italian witnesses. Her conduct, and the nature of the case made such evidence inevitable. It would be for the House to assess its value.

The Attorney-General announced that he would now call his witnesses. Before he could do so, however, Lord King wanted to know whether they would be liable, if it appeared that any of them had committed perjury, and could they be brought to trial; to which the Lord Chancellor replied that although the present proceedings were a little unusual (a typical British understatement if ever there was one) it was his opinion that this could be done.

Before the first witness was called to the Bar the Queen, who had not been present during the Attorney-General's opening speech, entered the House accompanied by Lady Anne Hamilton and took her seat in a chair within a few feet of the Bar in such a position as to enable her to confront the witnesses.

The Solicitor-General then called the first witness, Theodore Majocchi, and as soon as the Queen saw him take his place before the Bar she exclaimed in a piercing voice, according to the reports which appeared next morning in all the daily papers, "Theodore, Theodore!" Many peers and spectators who also heard her, however, were under the impression that what she called out was, "*Tradidore, tradidore!*" (Traitor, traitor!)

Whether she said Theodore or *tradidore* is of some consequence because of the use that was subsequently made of the incident by the prosecution to suggest that the Queen's reaction on seeing Majocchi enter as the first witness was a sign of her guilt. It is more reasonable to infer, however, and more consistent with the evidence given by this witness in the course of his cross-examination, that his treachery and ingratitude to a kind and indulgent mistress so mortified her as to provoke her into calling him a traitor.

One commentator on the trial compared the Queen's reaction to that of Julius Ceasar when he saw his old friend Brutus among his assassins, and quoted the famous lines from Mark Antony's funeral oration:

> For when the noble Caesar saw him stab,
> Ingratitude, more strong than traitor's arms,
> Quite vanquished him: then burst his mighty heart. . . .

The Solicitor-General then asked permission for the Marchese Nicolas Spinetto to be sworn in as an interpreter. He was then asked who had appointed him and replied that he had received his instructions from Mr. Planta of the Foreign Office and Mr. Maule, solicitor to the Treasury. Brougham told their Lordships that those were two sufficient reasons for his asking for a second interpreter to be sworn and this application was agreed to and Binetto Cohen was sworn in as interpreter on behalf of the Queen.

The Solicitor-General surprised everyone, when he began his examination of Majocchi by calling Pergami by his proper name instead of using the name Bergami as the Attorney-General had done throughout his opening speech. This was, presumably, because otherwise none of the witnesses would have known to whom he was referring.

Majocchi told the House that he first met Pergami in 1814 in the house of the Princess of Wales when he entered her service as a "livery servant or lackey". At that time Pergami used to have his meals at the table of the upper servants with Mr. Sicard, and the room in which he slept was close to the Princess's bedroom and was connected with it by a small corridor leading through a tiny closet. This was the same Sicard who had been in Caroline's service at Montague House and had given evidence in the Delicate Investigation.

Shortly after Majocchi began his employment on the Staff of the Princess, he said, Pergami was kicked by a horse and was confined to bed for a few days, during which time the witness slept in the closet at the far end of the corridor. On two occasions while he was sleeping there the witness saw Her Royal Highness pass through the corridor leading to Pergami's room during the night. She did so very quietly and as she passed the witness's bed she stopped to see whether he was awake or asleep and then proceeded to enter Pergami's room where she remained for about a quarter of an hour during which time he could hear them whispering.

This sounded most unlikely and a murmur of disbelief was heard throughout the House. At this stage an argument took place between the Solicitor-General and Brougham as to whether other witnesses should be allowed to remain in the House during the examination of a witness before they had themselves given evidence. Exclusion of witnesses was the general practice in all courts of justice and Brougham had no doubt that it would be adopted by their Lordships. The Lord Chancellor agreed that it should be done.

When the Solicitor-General said, in reply, that he hoped that Brougham would take equal care to ensure that his witnesses would also be excluded Brougham retaliated by saying that if all the Crown's witnesses were only going to give the kind of evidence which he had so far heard from Majocchi the defence would not bother to call any witnesses, at which there was much laughter.

Majocchi then described the sleeping accommodation at the hotel in Venice, but all he was able to say was that the bedrooms in which the Princess and Pergami slept were at opposite ends of a large drawing-room and that while they stayed in the hotel the Princess dined with him at the same table. When they moved from Milan to a villa on the shores of Lake Como the witness used to make Pergami's bed each morning and on some occasions it did not appear to have been slept in.

This evidence was exactly the opposite of what the Attorney-General had stated in his opening speech would be proved by his witnesses, namely that it was the Princess's bed which had not been slept in whereas there were signs that two persons had slept in Pergami's bed.

The examination of this witness continued until the end of the day's proceedings when the House adjourned until 10 a.m. the following day, but it was all extremely trivial and unconvincing. During his evidence the Queen spent most of her time in her waiting-room but when she left in her carriage and drove through St. James's Park and Hyde Park she was again greeted with loud cheers from the crowds who were waiting to see her pass.

The fifth day of the trial opened with the further examination of Majocchi, but nothing of any importance was elicited from him. He was supposed to be the Crown's chief witness, the mainbrace of its case, but his evidence had been very disappointing and in some particulars it had fallen far short of what the Attorney-General had predicted the evidence would be. If Majocchi were not believed that was an end of the case.

Now it was the Queen's turn and it did not take Brougham very long to demolish this witness entirely. He began with a preliminary skirmish, being guided chiefly by the first answers he received and by Majocchi's demeanour as a witness. After this had revealed weak spots in the enemy's defence, and there were plenty of them, the attack could begin.

As Brougham wrote in his autobiography,

I went to work as cautiously as possible, and after dealing with other topics I remembered an expression he had dropped in the former part of my cross-examination. It seemed to give me an opening and I went back and got an answer which made me quite secure. I indicated my sense of the advantage I had got by some gesture, which alarmed Denman who whispered words of caution; but I felt secure and then poured question after question into him and got him to repeat his *"non mi ricordo"* as often as I chose. The story among us was that my rising taller at the first opening the man gave me, put them in mind of the Duke of Wellington at Salamanca when he discovered that Marmont had left an opening in his line; and certainly the defeat of the Bill turned very much upon Majocchi's cross-examination. I mean the defeat as regards the opinion of our case by the Lords; for our strength against the Bill lay in the general demurrer which all men . . . made, namely that, admit everything true which is alleged against the Queen, after the treatment she has received ever since she came to England her husband had no right to the relief prayed by him and the punishment he sought against her.

Quite early in his cross-examination Majocchi began to give the answer "I don't remember" to almost every question. Brougham went through all the evidence the witness had given about the juxtaposition of the bedrooms, but whenever he tried to get a few more details they were very rarely forthcoming.

In the Princess's house in Naples where did William Austin sleep?—I do not remember.

Will you swear that he did not sleep in the next room to Her Royal Highness?—This I cannot remember.

What was the room next to the room in which Her Royal Highness slept?—I have seen no other [room].

Where did Doctor Holland, Her Royal Highness's physician sleep?—I do not remember.

Where did Hieronimus sleep?—I do not remember.

Where did Sir William Gell's servants sleep?—I do not remember.

Where did Louisa Demont, the maid, sleep?—I do not know.

Where did the other maids sleep?—I do not know.

Did you ever see Her Royal Highness go into Sir William Gell's room when he was ill?—I do not remember.

Or into Hieronimus's room?—I do not remember.

This was the same witness who remembered every detail about

the Princess and Pergami; where their bedrooms were, who slept in which bed, what arrangements were made at the various hotels where they stayed so that their rooms could be close together, how and when they breakfasted together and in what state of dress or undress. All these details which were, doubtless, contained in the Green Bag documents, had obviously been studied and learned by heart.

As the cross-examination proceeded the position became so farcical that after a series of *"non mi recordo"* the interpreter said that he found it most difficult to make himself understood. "The witness," he said, "is so confused."

At five o'clock the House adjourned with Majocchi still under cross-examination. He had had a gruelling time and when he left the witness stand he must have known that no one was prepared to believe him any longer.

On the sixth day of the trial, the Lord Chancellor having taken his seat on the Woolsack, Brougham renewed his cross-examination, during which twenty-nine questions were asked of the witness, of which fifteen were answered in the following words: "I do not know; I do not remember; I cannot recollect; I am not sure."

After a short argument between a number of peers, the Lord Chancellor and the interpreter about the correct translation of *"non mi recordo"*, Brougham was told that he could continue. He told their Lordships that he did not intend to question the witness further. "In this case," he said, "I have certainly no reason to ask him a single further question."

Very soon after the Solicitor-General had begun his re-examination of Majocchi the Queen, accompanied as usual by Lady Anne Hamilton, entered the Chamber. The peers rose and her Majesty bowed in return. She was noticed to be looking remarkably well. She took her seat near the Bar and followed the proceedings closely.

The re-examination did not take very long and it accomplished nothing. It was impossible to rehabilitate this witness in the eyes of the House and it might have been better if the Solicitor-General had declined to re-examine. He took great care, however, to ask questions which he felt quite certain Majocchi would not be likely to answer with the parrot cry of *"non mi recordo"*.

The Lord Chancellor then asked whether there was any noble Lord who had any questions to ask of the witness at the Bar. Several peers did ask questions and some of them were awkward and very much to the point. They certainly indicated that the majority of peers had already dismissed the evidence of the Crown's chief witness as unreliable.

At the close of the proceedings on the sixth day of the trial the Government and their Law Officers must have been more than somewhat depressed. With the exception of Louisa Demont, who was still to come, Majocchi was intended to be the most damaging witness against Caroline, but Brougham's cross-examination had destroyed his credibility and there was nothing the prosecution could do about it.

What the King felt that evening nobody knows, but he also had put complete faith in Majocchi as a witness and had actually received him at Carlton House on the very day of his father's funeral, so anxious was he to meet the man who was to rid him of Caroline.

Thomas Creevey, who attended the proceedings regularly, wrote daily about it to a friend and these letters provide an interesting running commentary of the scene. "Nothing," he wrote, "can be more triumphant for the Queen than this day. The truth is the Law Officers of the Crown are damnably overweighted by Brougham and Denman."

The effect on the general public of Majocchi's failure was also tremendous. From then on the King's witnesses, whose expenses must have cost the country many thousands of pounds, were called by everybody *"Non mi recordos"*.

On the seventh day of the trial only two witnesses were called but their evidence carried the case no further. One of them was Vincenzo Garguilo, who was master and owner of the *Palacca* in which Caroline had made her cruise around the eastern Mediterranean, when she was supposed to have allowed Pergami to take a bath in her cabin although not in her presence. The other was Francisco Birollo, who had been a cook in the Princess's household for about two years.

Immediately after Garguilo had finished his evidence and before Birollo began his, an application was made by Brougham to have Majocchi recalled immediately. Counsel said that he was making the application in consequence of a letter which he had just received. This had been written by a Mr. John Marsh of Gloucester to his friend Mr. Watts who lived in London. On receipt of the letter Mr. Watts had taken it to Alderman Wood who at once sent it to Brougham. The letter read as follows:

Gloucester, 23 August.
I know you to be a well-wisher of the Queen. The first witness called against her, I have every reason to believe, is a man who lived with Mr. Adam Hyatt, who brought him over from Italy. He always spoke in the highest terms of Her Majesty and said he had been offered a considerable sum of money and a place for life if he would appear against her. I can find very creditable people in Gloucester to whom he told this. I request you will make known these circumstances to Alderman Wood and some person may be sent from London to make the necessary inquiries here.

John Marsh

Brougham told the House that he wished to cross-examine Majocchi on this one subject only and the first question he wished to put was whether the witness had been in Bristol in the course of the last twelve to fourteen months. After a short argument the

Lord Chancellor advised their Lordships to allow the Queen's Attorney-General to cross-examine Majocchi, who was then called to the Bar. Although in the second half of this renewed cross-examination there were more than a few *"non mi recordos"* the answers to some of the questions were quite illuminating, and the first part of the cross-examination is, therefore, set out in full.

Were you or were you not at Bristol last year or in the course of this year?—I do not know this Bristol.

Were you at Gloucester?—Gloucester I know very well.

Were you in the service of a gentleman of the name of Hyatt?—Yes.

Did you ever declare to any person that the Princess of Wales was an excellent woman?—Yes, that the Princess was a good woman.

Did you ever declare that the conduct of the Princess was highly becoming?—Of her conduct I always said that she was a good woman but was surrounded by bad people.

Did you ever say that she was a prudent person and that you had never observed anything improper in her conduct?—*Non mi recordo.*

Did you ever say that the Princess of Wales behaved with propriety?—This I have never said.

Did you ever represent the Princess of Wales to any person in a stage coach as a much injured woman?—This I remember no more no than yes.

Majocchi consistently refused to admit, however, that he had ever told anyone that he had been asked to give evidence against the Queen and offered money and a permanent situation if he would do so. "I will lay down my life," he told Brougham, "if this be true." It is not surprising that he drew the line there, for he must have realized that the consequences of such an admission might be very serious.

25th August, the eighth day of the trial, was no better for the Government's supporters of the Bill than the sixth day had been. Captain Pechell and Captain Briggs, two British officers, were called and it was expected that their evidence would be most damaging to the Queen. The King's friends had for a long time been boasting about the evidence which Sir John Leach, who was in charge of the Milan Commission, had been collecting from various British officers.

Thomas Creevey, in one of his letters to Miss Ord, written after the House adjourned on the 25th, referred to the failure of these two officers to come up to the Crown's expectations:

> Our matters, so far in the day, stand much better than they did at the close of yesterday. The two Captains, Pechell and Briggs have been called and, so far from proving anything against the Queen, they have distinctly sworn there was not the slightest impropriety in the conduct of the Queen during the period she was on board their ships.
>
> The fact of Pergami having come the first time as servant and afterwards sitting at table on board one of those ships was, of course, proved; but everybody knew it before and it does not signify a damn. . . . The discovery of this day, viz that Captains Briggs and Pechell were to be the only English witnesses produced against the Queen, was most agreeable and unexpected to me because of a conversation which had passed between the Duke of Wellington and myself on the subject. The night after I made my speech in the House of Commons . . . I saw the Duke at the Argyle Rooms, who, with his usual frankness came to me and said: "Well Creevey, so you gave us a blast last night. Have you seen Leach since?"
>
> Then we talked about the approaching trial with the most perfect freedom, and upon my saying that foreign evidence would find very few believers in this country, he said, "Oh, but we have a great many English witnesses—officers."

The next witness called was Pietro Cuichi, who was supposed to prove, amongst other things, that when the Princess was staying at an inn in Trieste of which Cuichi was the landlord, her bedroom and that of Pergami were only separated by the dining-room into which both bedrooms led.

What Cuichi did not say, however, was that before Pergami could reach the dining-room he had to pass through another bedroom in which his sister, Contessa d'Oldi, slept. Nor was the Contessa called to say that during the night she had seen her brother pass through her room on the way to the Princess or vice versa.

The next witness called was Barbara Kress, who before her marriage had been a chambermaid at the Post Inn at Karlsruhe and remembered the Princess staying there and occupying a bedroom which had a communicating door to the dining-room. One evening, at about seven, Kress had to go to Pergami's room with some water. She entered the room, which was not locked, and saw Pergami in bed and the Princess sitting on the edge of the bed. Pergami had his arm round the Princess's neck. She noticed that it was white and she agreed with the suggestion that this could probably be explained by the fact that he was, at the time, wearing a shirt. The Princess, however, was fully dressed and when the chambermaid entered she jumped up.

At this stage of the evidence the interpreter explained that the literal translation of what the witness had just said was that the Princess "got up, or rose", which was not quite the same thing. This led to a long argument about the efficiency of the interpretation and it was suggested that the second interpreter should be sworn in to check the official interpreter. When questioned a second time Frau Kress repeated what she had said the first time and the interpreter translated the words used as "she got up".

The House then adjourned until the following day when the chambermaid gave further evidence to the effect that when she made Pergami's bed on another occasion she discovered that the sheets were stained. Again, however, there was some doubt about the interpretation of the word used by the witness and it was agreed that the correct translation should have been "soiled".

Although the Solicitor-General tried hard to get the witness to amplify this part of her evidence he failed dismally so Brougham, perhaps wisely, did not pursue the matter any further in his cross-examination.

This kind of evidence, this determination of the Crown to leave no stone unturned to blacken the Queen's character was having an effect quite different from what the supporters of the Bill hoped. As the trial proceeded the chances that the Bill would be passed by the House became more and more remote, unless, of course, their Lordships decided to vote on party lines.

When the House met again on 29th August Brougham asked permission for the Queen's counsel to be allowed to cross-examine witnesses after the examination-in-chief, to such an extent that they thought proper, with liberty to call back the witnesses later for such further cross-examination as they might desire.

Barbara Kress, therefore, was then recalled and further cross-examined by Brougham. The first part of the cross-examination appears to have been an attempt to suggest that she had been promised a large sum of money if she came to England to give this evidence. It achieved little success, however, for she would only admit that she was told she would receive due compensation. Remaining questions were no more successful and produced nothing of any value to either side. Frau Kress seems to have been an exceptionally stupid woman, but when she said that she did not understand a question it was not always because she did not know how to answer it.

On the following day, 30th August, after three or four more witnesses had been called by the Crown to give trivial evidence which carried the Crown's case no further, the great moment arrived and Louisa Demont was called to the Bar and was then examined by the Solicitor-General. She described how it was that Willikins ceased to sleep in the same room as his adopted mother and how Pergami was allotted a bedroom which had a communicating passage and a small closet between it and the Princess's room.

The witness then stated that during the time they were in Naples Pergami slept in his own room but she frequently saw him in the Princess's room when she was also in the room "assisting H.R.H. to make her toilette." On some of these occasions Willikins was also present. He was then about twelve years old.

She also said that on a number of occasions when she went to the Princess's bedroom to make up the large bed it appeared as though two people had slept in it, which was, of course, in complete contradiction to what Majocchi had said, namely, that the Princess's bed appeared not to have been slept in whereas there were signs that two persons had slept in his bed.

The more the evidence of these two witnesses is examined the more unreliable it becomes. Not only were the two stories diametrically opposed but Majocchi's story was self-contradictory. If the Princess left her room, entered Pergami's room, stayed there for only fifteen minutes and then went back to her room, where did she sleep the rest of the night, having regard to the fact that Majocchi next morning found that her bed had not been slept in? Even the Solicitor-General did not suggest that she had spent the remainder of the night on the bedroom floor.

This witness then went on to describe the sleeping arrangements when they were all living in Genoa. The Princess's room had two communicating rooms, one on either side. Pergami slept in one of them and Demont in the other. In the morning Her Royal Highness would call her maid into the room and, Demont swore, "More often than not the bed appeared not to have been slept in."

Having regard to the fact that Caroline knew from the moment she left England that she was being spied upon day and night and that she must have realized that some of her domestic staff were there for that purpose, it is difficult, if not impossible, to believe that she would have regularly spent the night in Pergami's bed with her own maid a stone's throw away, and in the morning called Kress into her bedroom without even bothering to ruffle the sheets.

Although the examination of this witness by the Solicitor-General lasted for almost a day and a half, most of the evidence given, apart from that already mentioned, was of a very trivial nature. She had seen the Princess and Pergami *sitting* on the sofa together; in a canoe on Lake Como; walking arm in arm with him in the garden at the Villa D'Este; drinking together, and a number of other harmless things. Demont also stated that although the Princess often called him *"mon cher ami"* and addressed him as *"tu"*, he always called her Princess.

This was hardly the kind of evidence required to prove a charge of adulterous intercourse, and at the end of Demont's examination many of their Lordships must have been wondering whether the Queen had not been speaking the truth when she told someone that the only man with whom she had ever committed adultery was the husband of Mrs. Fitzherbert!

On Friday 1st September the cross-examination of Louisa Demont began and Brougham entrusted this very important task to Mr. T. Williams, one of Her Majesty's three junior counsel. No one could have done it better. By the end of the day, although her cross-examination was not quite finished, she left the witness stand greatly discredited.

Thomas Creevey, who was in the House all day, in a letter written to Miss Ord said:

The chienne Demont turns out everything one could wish in her cross-examination. Her letters have been produced written to her sister living still in the Queen's service. . . . They contain every kind of panegyric upon the Queen, and she often writes of a journal or diary she has kept of everything that has occurred during the whole of her service and travels with the Queen—the object of such journal being, as she said, to do the Queen justice and to show how she was received and applauded wherever she went.

Mr. Williams began by asking the witness whether it was not a fact that she had been living in England for the last thirteen months under the name of Colombier, to which she answered "Yes". She also admitted that after being in the Princess's service for just over three years she was dismissed in 1817 for saying something which she afterwards admitted to be false. After her dismissal she did not take up any further employment until after her arrival in England in July 1819.

From most of counsel's questions during the early part of her cross-examination she took evasive action. First she would answer, "I do not recollect having done so," and on being asked whether she would *swear* that she had not done so, her reply was always, "I will not swear but I do not recollect it".

The Solicitor-General must have begun to realize that his "storm troops" were not doing too well as he kept interrupting the Queen's counsel and complaining of the form in which a question had just been put. In no case were any of the questions put improperly, but as the Solicitor-General was allowed by the Lord Chancellor to get away with his objection every time, it was obviously worthwhile his continuing to interrupt whenever possible, as each time he did so, Demont, who was under great pressure from Mr. Williams, was given a little breathing space, which must have been a great relief to her.

The most vital part of her cross-examination, however, began when counsel suggested that she was very short of money before she came to England and that about six months after she was dismissed from the Princess's service someone approached her in order to find out what she had to say with respect to her former mistress. Demont fenced with counsel over these questions for several minutes, although she finally had to admit that she had been approached but rather later than counsel had suggested. The effect of her prevarication, however, cannot have been lost on anyone present.

When the House met on the following day, 2nd September, Mr. Williams said that with the permission of the House he proposed to read two letters which had been written by the witness Demont. The first was addressed to Mademoiselle Mariette Bron at Pesaro and dated, Colombier, 8th February 1818. The second was addressed to H.R.H. the Princess of Wales.

When the first letter was read out by counsel it was then seen to be the same letter about which the witness had been cross-examined earlier and of which she pretended that she could not remember any of the details—a letter which stated that while Demont was having some refreshment at her aunt Clara's an unknown man had brought her a letter. Counsel now asked if this was true and, after a lot more prevarication, for this witness seemed to be constitutionally incapable of telling the simple truth, she admitted that such a letter was delivered to her and she wished to explain it. This explanation, which was later proved to be palpably false, was put forward with the object of showing that the flattering things which the witness had said about her former mistress were not genuine and were written for an entirely different reason.

"I wrote to my sister several times," she told counsel, "and always in these letters I spoke much about Her Royal Highness because I knew they would be intercepted. At that time I had decided to leave Switzerland and go to England and I was afraid that the Princess would dismiss my sister. I knew that since I had left the service of Her Royal Highness she had always feared that I would speak against her and as I knew that she would read these letters I wanted to convince her that I would not speak against her even if I went to England and that even money would not tempt me. I did this in the hope that she would not dismiss my sister from her service."

After that nothing could really rehabilitate this witness, neither

her re-examination by the Solicitor-General nor her examination by a number of Tory peers who were strong supporters of the Bill for purely political reasons. A good deal of what she had told the House about the conduct of the Princess and Pergami may still have left some suspicion in the minds of some, but no reasonable person could be so certain of her truthfulness as to be prepared to act on it.

The House only sat for six more days before they adjourned for a little more than three weeks in order that the Queen's counsel might have time to prepare her defence. On the first four days further witnesses were called and the Solicitor-General summed-up in support of the Bill. Only one of the witnesses contributed anything new to the case and even his evidence covered mostly the same ground as that of Majocchi and Demont. That the Crown thought it necessary to call a baker to say that he was once in the kitchen at the Villa D'Este and saw Pergami take a spoonful of polenta, put half of it into the Princess's mouth and then the remainder in his own mouth, only shows how desperately short they were of evidence to support the charges.

Nor was the Solicitor-General's summing-up very impressive. He went through the evidence in considerable detail, but had to admit that Majocchi was a witness "unworthy of belief" and that the facts to which he had sworn were not directly confirmed by the witness Demont.

A strange point of which he made special mention was the evidence of Giuseppe Sacchi that during the whole of the Princess's journey through Germany and the Tyrol, Sacchi had stated, the greatest anxiety had been shown by Her Royal Highness to avoid the English upon every occasion; the first question asked on arrival at any inn or hotel was, "are there any English of rank here?" If the answer was yes, the party immediately went somewhere else. Which of all the allegations made against the Queen this was supposed to prove it is difficult to conceive, but whether guilty or innocent, it was more than understandable, after the treatment she had received ever since she first set foot in England, that the Queen might not want to be seen dead in the same ditch with any compatriots of her royal husband.

In the last few words of his speech the Solicitor-General laid bare the complete injustice of the procedure adopted by the Government at the bequest of their King in order to get rid of his wife. He hoped that in conclusion he might be allowed to say, and he said it from the bottom of his heart and with the utmost sincerity, that he devoutly wished that Her Royal Highness would establish to the satisfaction of their Lordships, and every individual in the country, her full and unsullied innocence. He apparently had forgotten that, if justice was to be done, it was for the Crown to establish her guilt, and not for her to establish her innocence.

At the close of this speech the House adjourned so that Brougham could decide whether or not they required an adjournment in order to prepare the defence. On Saturday 9th September, after hearing Brougham's wishes, the House adjourned until Tuesday 3rd October when the Bill would be further considered.

The Government was apparently quite determined not to let Brougham open his case at once, but when he was allowed an adjournment of more than three weeks the House of Lords were not at all pleased. As Creevey wrote, "You can form no conception of the rage of the Lords at Brougham fixing this time: it interferes with everything,—pheasant shooting, Newmarket etc.!"

During the proceedings of the House since the commencement of the second reading of the Bill the King must have been watching them with some uneasiness. Just before the House adjourned the Prime Minister wrote to give His Majesty a report of how everything was going. It was difficult to assess, he wrote, what the real effect of the evidence had been upon their Lordships. Parts of it had made a considerable impression in the minds of peers who were already ganged-up against the Queen but two of the most material witnesses had been badly shaken regarding their credit and character. Lord Liverpool was not prepared to prophesy about the result, particularly as he understood that the Queen had some important witnesses including Demont's sister, Mariette Bron, and two officers of the British Army.

The Prime Minister also warned the King that the opposition were determined to make a party question of the trial and would "strain every nerve and raise every doubt, however futile" to acquit the Queen. The main object of his letter, however, was to call attention to the last four lines of the Bill which dealt with divorce and, by inference, would enable the King to marry again. He told the King that he had been in constant touch with most of the peers, including the Bishops, and this had convinced him that there was little chance of that part of the Bill being passed in the House of Lords, and no possibility whatsoever that it would pass through the Commons. As far as the House of Lords was concerned this proved to be a wrong prediction because on 8th November the divorce clause was retained in the Bill by a majority of sixty-seven.

The Prime Minister also thought it necessary to remind the King that the proof required of adultery would be far stricter if a divorce were to follow than if the Bill was limited to the degradation of the Queen as unfit, because of her conduct, to share and enjoy the rights and privileges of Queen Consort. He therefore asked the King to give him authority to offer to give up the divorce clause before the defence commenced, should the King's Ministers think it desirable. Such an offer would, probably, conciliate the House and it would make it very difficult, if not impossible, for the defence then to bring up "the distressing subject of recrimination." He also thought it was preferable that His Majesty should make this concession rather than have it extorted from him, and it would also ensure considerable support from the public.

The King, in his reply, told the Prime Minister that this was not a decision he could make without serious consideration and this would take time. He would have to discuss the suggestion with Lord Liverpool personally before he could accept such a compromise.

Eventually, after a meeeting with some of his Ministers, the King regretfully agreed to the suggestion and wrote to tell him so. He expressed the hope, however, that the Prime Minister would protect the King's honour and not yield to political expediency.

On 3rd October the House reassembled to resume the second reading of the Bill and the proceedings began with Brougham's opening speech for the defence, a speech which did more than anything else to kill the Bill.

He began by expressing the hope that the Queen's innocence would be realized before the proceedings ended and that it would not be prejudiced by his unworthy handling of the case. There was, however, one thing in his favour. Public opinion had already decided on the case and he had nothing to fear but the consequences of perjury.

He then dealt with all the evidence which had been given by the witnesses of the Crown. Although there had been a great deal of mud slinging and some of the mud would certainly stick, it did not substantiate, beyond doubt, any of the charges contained in the Bill.

The witnesses Majocchi and Demont stood apart from the rest of the witnesses; they were the main witnesses on whom the whole case depended. All the others could do was corroborate these two witnesses in some material particular. Both of them, however, were gravely shaken under cross-examination and their credit virtually destroyed. The reason why Demont prevaricated so obstinately about her handwriting was that her evidence had been given in utter ignorance that her letters were still in existence and could be produced in evidence to contradict her. As Brougham said, had she known that those letters were available and that their contents were known to the King's advisers "their Lordships would never have heard of her and she would have been shipped off again as many other bribed witnesses had been who were even less worthy of credit than those who had been called."

Some of the disgusting evidence was also the most incredible, because it was impossible to believe that the Princess and Pergami, unless they were quite mad, would have dreamed of doing some of the things they were said to have been seen doing, in circumstances in which they were almost certain to be caught in the act.

Brougham's speech ended with the following peroration:

Such, my Lords, now before you, is the evidence in support of this measure; evidence inadequate to prove a debt, impotent to deprive of a right, ridiculous to convict of the lowest offence, scandalous if brought forward to support a charge of the highest nature which the law knows, monstrous to ruin the honour, to blast the name of an English Queen.

My Lords, I pray you to pause, I do earnestly beseech you to take heed. You are standing on the brink of a precipice, then beware! It will go forth as your judgement, if sentence shall go against the Queen; but it will be the only judgement you ever pronounced which instead of reaching its object, will return and bound back on those who gave it.

Save the country, my Lords, from the horrors of catastrophe. Save yourselves from this peril. Rescue that country, of which you are the ornaments, but in which you can flourish no longer, when severed from the people, than the blossom when cut off from the roots and the stem of the tree. Save that country that you may continue to adorn it. Save the Crown which is in jeopardy, the aristocracy which is shaken. Save the altar which must stagger with the blow that rends its kindred throne.

You have said, my Lords, you have willed, the Church and King have willed, that the Queen should be deprived of its solemn service. She has, instead of that solemnity, the heartfelt prayers of the people.

She needs no prayers of mine, but I do here pour forth my humble supplications at the throne of mercy that that mercy may be poured down upon the people in a larger measure than the merits of their rulers may deserve and that your hearts may be turned to justice.

Sir Fitzjames Stephen once said, "eloquence of the past resembles nothing so much as mouldy wedding cake," and the above peroration certainly sounds very flowery to modern ears. Nevertheless, it made a great impression on the House, and Lord Erskine, himself no mean orator, left the chamber in tears, during the short adjournment which followed, and many other noble Lords stood about in groups in the lobbies discussing it.

Brougham is supposed to have been in two minds whether or not to call any witnesses at all in defence of the Queen and, had this been a trial before a jury in an ordinary criminal court, that might have been the best course to have adopted. Instead of calling any evidence he would have merely submitted that there was no case to answer. Very different considerations, however, applied to this case. The House of Lords in no way resembled a jury, chosen haphazardly from a register of householders and all liable to be challenged for cause. Had the same principle been applicable to this jury of peers all those of the same political persuasion as the Government of the day would have been challengeable on the ground of prejudice, for the Bill which was before the House was a political measure. But apart from that consideration, if no witness had been called in the Queen's defence, the King, his Ministers and his friends would have claimed, without doubt, that the reason for not calling any witnesses was that the defence dare not risk it. In any event, the Queen herself was not willing to let the matter go by default and insisted that witnesses should be called.

That was, no doubt, why Brougham eventually decided that they should be called, and why he had dealt with it earlier in his speech and had told the House that the evidence which had been given against Her Majesty in support of the charges did not call upon him to make any rebuttal.

He also frightened the Government and its supporters by saying that although he did not at that stage of the proceedings intend to utter one whisper against the conduct of "Her Majesty's illustrious Consort" he would not hesitate to "resort to such a course and fearlessly perform his duty" should it become necessary.

The House knew perfectly well what he meant by that. The whole story of the King's unpleasant and disreputable amours and his marriage to Mrs. Fitzherbert would then have been blazoned all over the country and would have done irreparable harm, not only to the King but to the monarchy itself. It would, also, have been a defence to any legal claim for a divorce which was still part of the Bill.

After Mr. Williams, one of the Queens' junior counsel, had with their permission addressed their Lordships he called a number of highly respectable witnesses, all of whom had either been on the Princess's staff or had met her during her absence abroad. One of them, the Bishop of Pesaro, testified that, during the three years when she was living there, there had never been the slightest report or even rumour that could be injurious to her honour or reputation. He told the House that had there been any scandal connected with her household it certainly could not have remained concealed from his court. A large number of other witnesses holding important positions in various parts of Italy in which the Princess had been living gave similar evidence.

Lady Charlotte Lindsay, who was one of the Princess's Ladies of the Bedchamber when Her Royal Highness was living in Naples and Rome, swore that she had never seen any impropriety of conduct between the Princess and Pergami nor had she noticed anything to make her suspect that there was any such conduct. When cross-examined by the Solicitor-General she would not swear that she had never seen Pergami take the Princess's arm but if she did it was certainly not done in such a way as to give rise to any suspicion that there was undue intimacy.

Sir William Gell, who had been Chamberlain in the Princess's household from the time she went abroad until shortly before her cruise to the eastern Mediterranean, testified, and his evidence was not shaken in cross-examination, that Pergami's conduct was that of a gentleman and that he (Sir William) had never observed anything in Pergami's conduct towards the Princess different from the conduct of any English member of the staff, except, perhaps, that he was more attentive.

But the most important evidence was given by Sicard, who had been in Her Royal Highness's household for more than twenty years. It was important because it explained how it was that in Naples Pergami was allotted a room not far from that of the Princess. It was, in fact, Sicard who, on Gell's instructions, engaged Pergami as courier, on the recommendation of the Marchese Ghisiliari in whose service he had previously been. Two or three nights later Sicard moved Pergami to another room. The room was chosen principally because it had a glass door which led to the garden and was not safe, and, therefore, Sicard "thought it right that a male servant should sleep in it". Unlike Majocchi and Demont, Sicard was not shaken in cross-examination and throughout his evidence gave every appearance of being a thoroughly reliable witness.

During the next few days a number of other witnesses were called by the defence and dealt with various aspects of the evidence given by Majocchi and Demont. By the time they had finished the Crown's case was even further demolished.

On 13th October an application was made by Brougham to recall one of the Crown's witnesses, Rastelli. It had become clear by then that Rastelli had committed perjury, and as the Attorney-General had promised that any such witnesses would be prosecuted there was an uproar when he announced that Rastelli had, without the knowledge of the Law Officers, been sent to Milan with despatches. He had been ordered to return immediately. Brougham protested at this, because, he said, the nature of Rastelli's cross-examination was such as would lead any reasonable person to suspect that it would be contradicted.

Lord Holland also severely criticized the Crown for allowing this to happen and said that if their Lordships allowed themselves to be thus dragged through the mire they would place the country's institutions in the utmost jeopardy and danger. In his opinion a prima facie case had already been made out of the existence of a conspiracy to prevent the course of justice and the House would do well to get rid of the disgust and fatigue of this infamous proceeding.

These were strong words and they left the Prime Minister with no alternative but to get up and rebut the accusation. He admitted that someone was seriously to blame but neither he, the Attorney-General, nor the Solicitor-General knew anything about this. He was sure that whoever had been responsible for Rastelli's departure had acted from the highest motives.

Lord Liverpool had fallen back on the politician's age-long device of professing ignorance when to admit knowledge would be most embarrassing, but he was not allowed to get away with it too easily. Lord Lansdowne thought that their Lordships should always have the power to recall any witness whose evidence was suspect. He poured ridicule on the reason given by the Attorney-General for Rastelli's absence and said that it was incumbent on their Lordships to do all they could to repair the error.

The Lord Chancellor also did what he could to cover up for the Crown, professing, at the same time, his complete ignorance. He said that it was most unfortunate, but an error of judgment rather than "an error of intention".

But this did not stop several other peers joining in the protest. Lord Carnarvon maintained that these proceedings made the

House of Lords "an object of execration to every Englishman and of contempt to the rest of Europe". Lord Alvanley wanted to know the name of the person who had sent Rastelli to Milan and asked whether, by any chance, he was one of the Milan Commissioners, an awkward question to which, of course, he received no reply; and Lord Grey disagreed with the Lord Chancellor's excuse that it was merely an error of judgment. He thought it highly iniquitous.

Creevey, as usual, had some lively comment to make and wrote, "Here's a breeze of the first order! The last witness having ended Rastelli was called back when, behold, it turned out that he had been sent *out of the country* instead of staying and being indicted for perjury. . . . Liverpool admits it was scandalous to send him away but that it was unknown to the Government!"

Although the Prime Minister had not deigned to answer Lord Alvanley's pertinent question the mystery, if there were any, was cleared up by a witness who was called just before the House rose. His name was Powell and Lord Alvanley's suspicions had been well founded, for in answer to the first question put to him by Lord Grey the witness admitted that he had been employed under the Milan Commission and was then assisting agents in support of the Bill. He had suggested to the Foreign Office that Rastelli should be sent on this mission to Milan. He had, however, given Rastelli firm instructions to return on or before 3rd of October but had since heard that he was too ill to travel.

So the King's Ministers managed to evade personal responsibility by passing it on to a civil servant. It is not customary for a Minister to do this and it is not to Lord Liverpool's credit that he did not have the courage to shoulder the blame himself. The House, however, was not left with any illusions and there can have been few peers who were not convinced that Rastelli's illness was diplomatic. As Powell well knew that an indictment for perjury would later be made against Rastelli he must have realized that it was most unlikely that this Italian would return to face such a charge and that it would not be possible to extradite him.

As the proceedings of the House of Lords, since the second reading of the Bill began, had received wide coverage in *The Times* and in all the other newspapers, the whole of England had been avidly following the trial and its reaction had not been favourable to the King, to put it mildly. The King himself was incensed at the way the trial was going and dare not show his face outside Carlton House because of the public hostility. The crowds assembled outside kept shouting, "Nero's hotel, let's burn it down," and it was then that the first police force was formed. Robert Peel, watching the crowds moving along the streets in the vicinity of Carlton House and threatening to overthrow the monarchy, wondered whether, if the situation got out of hand, the army could be relied upon, for the troops were very much on the Queen's side. He suggested the formation of a regular police force directly under the Crown. His friends thought it an excellent idea and suggested that its members should be called Peelers, the name by which the police in London were known for some time.

The King, however, was not only furious at the way things were going. He was also frightened because he knew only too well what Brougham had meant when he alluded, in his opening speech, to the fact that unless there was later some reason which gave him no option, he intended to draw a veil over the period between the Queen's first arrival in England and her departure in 1814, but that he could not do so if he found later that this would prejudice the Queen's case. Should it become necessary he would not hesitate to make a personal attack on the King whatever the consequences might be.

The Queen's legal advisers had abundant evidence which would have proved a strong case against the King, but Brougham thought, at that stage, that it would never have induced His Majesty to give up the Bill. The King knew that everyone in society knew of his relationship with Lady Jersey and it would make no difference if it were to be proved at the Bar of the House.

Had it been necessary the real ground of defence which Brougham would have brought forward would have been nothing less than impeaching the King's title by proving that he had forfeited the Crown. He had married a Roman Catholic while heir-apparent and this was declared by the Act of Settlement to be a forfeiture of the Crown, "as if he were naturally dead". Brougham was not at that time in possesion of all the evidence to prove this, as he became later; but he was now confident that he had enough evidence to prove the fact. Mrs. Fitzherbert's uncle, Mr. Errington, who was present at the marriage, which took place in his house, was still alive, and although he would have had a right to refuse to reply to a question, an affirmative answer to which would have incriminated him, it was almost certain, in Brougham's opinion, that on Mrs. Fitzherbert's behalf he would have waived the protection and given his testimony to prove the marriage. Even his refusal to answer such a question would have left the conviction in everyone's mind that the marriage did take place.

There was, in fact, ample evidence in existence which would have enabled Brougham to prove that the marriage had taken place without involving Errington. Mrs. Fitzherbert had in her possession a will made by the Prince of Wales in her favour and signed in his own hand in which she was referred to as "his dear wife". Brougham had actually obtained a copy of this will from a Mrs. Dawson Damer, who was the adopted daughter and was only too pleased to help in any way in defending the reputation of her adoptive mother, of whom she was very fond.

How far Brougham could have gone in proving all this it is impossible to know, for it was many years before all the evidence was disclosed to the public. The mere suggestion of it, however, would have been quite enough to create a terrible scandal, if no more, and it would, surely, have been the end of the Bill. No wonder George was worried.

On 24th October Denman began his summing-up for the defence, which lasted for the best part of two days. It was extremely forceful and telling and completely demolished the Crown's evidence. It had only one blemish and that was an unfortunate gaffe which marred his peroration. He quoted Our Lord's words to the woman taken in adultery, "Go and sin no more". Having regard to the fact that the whole object of his speech had been to prove that the Queen had not sinned at all, nothing could have been more inept.

This was too good for London's lampooners to miss, and it was not long before the following verse was current in all the taverns:

> Gracious lady, we implore,
> Go away and sin no more,
> And if that effort be too great,
> Go away at any rate.

On 27th October, the forty-third day of the trial, the Attorney-General replied to the defence and was followed by the Solicitor-General. In *The Times* of the following day one of the leader writers stated that there had been a prevalent opinion that the failure of the charges against the Queen being now clear there would be no point in the Law Officers of the Crown being called upon to attempt to reply. It was thought that they would have been glad to be excused. What their feelings may have been it is impossible to say but the effect of their speeches was not great and did nothing to re-establish their case.

The so-called trial having now ended all that remained was for the House to vote on the second reading of the Bill, but before a division was called a number of peers spoke after the Lord Chancellor had first addressed them.

Notwithstanding all that had been heard, he said, the only

question for the House to judge was whether the Bill should or should not be read a second time. Suggestions had been made regarding certain amendments which would alter its nature (this referred to the divorce clause) but these had nothing to do with their Lordships' decision.

No one should vote for the second reading unless he thought that the substantial parts of the Preamble had been proved and especially that an adulterous intercourse had taken place. He did not intend to go into the evidence in any great detail as it was not part of his duty to sum-up like a judge in a court of law, but it was his duty to state his opinion and, in giving it, to refer to those parts of the evidence on which that opinion was founded.

He told them, however, that they must observe the great principles of British justice (which must have sounded strange in the Queen's ears), namely to consider the accused innocent until proved guilty and to pronounce the Queen innocent unless *"perfectly satisfied"* that she had been proved guilty.

One would have thought that no reasonable man could have been perfectly satisfied of her guilt after the evidence of witnesses like Majocchi and Demont, yet in the division on the second reading of the Bill which took place at the end of this debate 123 peers voted for it and it was carried by a majority of twenty-eight.

The question which the Lord Chancellor asked himself, before deciding how to vote, was "does the evidence which stands unsuspected in support of the Bill and uncontradicted by the defence evidence sustain the allegation of an adulterous intercourse or does it not?" Again, it is difficult to understand how Lord Eldon, experienced lawyer and judge, could have answered that question in the affirmative particularly as the standard of belief which he had already set himself, and the other peers, was that they should be "perfectly satisfied".

When, however, he came to deal with the evidence itself he was in some difficulty and he never even mentioned the evidence of Majocchi or Demont, although he said that it should not be thought that both these witnesses on many occasions had not told the truth.

When he sat down he was followed by Lord Erskine, a former Lord Chancellor, who, it will be remembered, had presided over the Delicate Investigation and had cleared the Princess of Wales, as she then was, of all the serious charges brought against her. He already knew the kind of persecution which the Princess had undergone, ever since her husband left her for Mrs. Fitzherbert after the birth of Charlotte, and he naturally viewed the Bill with some suspicion. He told the House that he felt bound to say that Lord Eldon had not exhibited the same impartiality which he had recommended to others.

Lord Erskine had always been of the opinion that when the Queen's name had been omitted from the liturgy, almost before the last breath had left the late King's body, she had been unjustly deprived of the prayers of the Church by the agency of the new King's Ministers. The Lord Chancellor, Lord Erskine said, would appear to have forgotten that incident, otherwise he could never have said that in England no one could be considered guilty until it had been proved and that no opinion ought to be expressed against an accused prior to the trial.

Before he could finish his speech, however, he was taken ill and fell "senseless on the table". It was not realized that his indisposition was serious and the House adjourned for a quarter of an hour to give him time to recover. He had not, however, recovered by that time and the debate had to go on without him. Now that poor Erskine was, at least temporarily, out of the way the Lord Chancellor rose to say that he could not let the debate go further without saying that Lord Erskine, whose absence and indisposition he regretted, had mistaken what he meant when he (Erskine) said that Lord Eldon had overlooked many of the points in the case.

What the Lord Chancellor meant to say was that in the points and cases upon which he had commented he saw enough for his own judgment.

It is always unfortunate to have to say in public that one did not mean what one said, although it is still done almost every day by politicians from Prime Ministers downwards. In this particular instance it was quite clear that what the Lord Chancellor had said could only have meant one thing to any reasonable person and that was exactly what Lord Erskine had taken it to mean. In his explanation Lord Eldon completely gave the game away by saying that the evidence that he had mentioned was enough for *his* judgment.

During the remainder of this last debate on the second reading there were more who spoke against the Bill than in favour of it although there was by then very little doubt that the Government would get a majority even though it might not be a large one.

In a letter dated 2nd November, the same day on which Erskine was taken ill, Creevey wrote:

> Eldon began this morning and it was expected he would have made a great masterly judicial summing-up; instead of which he spoke for an hour and a quarter only and a more feeble argument for his own vote I never heard in my life. . . . Erskine followed and had spoken for about three quarters of an hour when he fainted away and was carried out of the House, since when that villain Lauderdale has been speaking.

"That villain Lauderdale" came up to expectations for he made a very long speech and examined the whole of the evidence in great detail. Unlike Eldon, who was only able to rely on parts of it—enough to satisfy an easy conscience and vote for the Bill—Lauderdale swallowed it all hook, line and sinker, going so far as to say that in all its material parts the evidence of Majocchi and Demont was unimpeached. His final exhortation was a little too much even for some of his own colleagues, namely that they should vote for the second reading in order to protect the morals of their wives and children. Everyone knew, whatever their political colour, that the last thing the Bill was about was the protection of either public or private morals.

A number of peers who spoke later criticized Lauderdale's hypocritical speech, including Lord Grosvenor, who had some hard things to say about the Archbishop of Canterbury and the Lord Chancellor. It was generally understood that on his accession the King had asked the Archbishop to come and see him with the book of Common Prayer and had ordered the Primate to erase Caroline's name from the liturgy. Lord Grosvenor did not know whether those were the facts but in those circumstances, if he had been the Archbishop, he would have thrown the book in the face of a King who commanded him to do an act which was contrary to law, to humanity and to justice.

Similarly had Lord Grosvenor been the Lord Chancellor he would, sooner than set the seal of office to such a Command, have dashed the seal to pieces at his feet and thrown away the trammels of his office rather than remain any longer in the service of such a King.

His exhortation to the House was very different from that of Lauderdale. Rather than pass the Bill to protect the morals of their wives and children Lord Grosvenor thought that in respect of a woman who had been "so injured, so unquestionably persecuted and oppressed" they should not exhibit to their wives and daughters the "sad spectacle of oppression which the Queen would present were she to become the victim of this Bill". They should judge this measure as they themselves expected to be judged.

When the division was taken on 6th November, there voted contents 123, non-contents ninety-five, majority for the second reading twenty-eight; but this was no victory for the King or for his Government, for everyone knew that the Bill would never pass through the House of Commons, if ever it reached there.

The voting had little to do with the merits of the case, otherwise the Bill would have been defeated by quite a substantial majority. Many peers voted solely for political reasons and it must have been a relief to those whose political sympathies, on this occasion, coincided with the course of justice.

An analysis of twenty-eight peers who voted in support of the Bill and accounted for the majority is not without interest.

Princes of the blood holding high office at His Majesty's pleasure	2
Cabinet Ministers	9
Peers holding offices under the Crown	13
The Archbishop of Canterbury	1
Three Peers who were present during the presentation of the prosecution's case but not in attendance to hear the defence	3
	28

When the House met next morning the Prime Minister attempted to carry out the promise which he had made to some of the Bishops that he would get rid of the divorce clause in the Bill, and the House went into Committee.

Before proposing that this clause should no longer stand part of the Bill, he proposed one or two absurdly trivial amendments typical of the Government's attitude ever since the Bill had been introduced. Firstly it was proposed that the name Bartolomo Pergami should be altered to Bartolomo Bergami. The orignial spelling of his name in the Preamble of the Bill was, in fact, one of the few statements in it which could be substantiated for the simple reason that it was his real name. One or two other amendments equally trivial were also proposed and accepted.

But it was when the Chairman of the House in Committee came to the divorce clause that the Government got a shock. The opposition, who were out to destroy the Bill in any event, supported the retention of this clause, believing, and they were later proved to be right, that with the divorce clause still in the Bill the majority obtained by the Government on the second reading would be considerably reduced on the third reading.

Friday 10th November was to see the end of the Bill. It was the third reading, and after a fairly short debate it was passed by a majority of only nine. While the division was taking place Brougham was standing by Croker, who had taken a very active part in the affair. When the result of the division was announced Brougham said, "there is an end of your Bill!" "Why?" Croker asked. "Because," Brougham replied, "the majority is the number of Ministers and high officers in this House, and it will never do to pass such a Bill by their votes."

By this time, however, the Government had seen the red light and the Prime Minister rose at once and said that he could not be ignorant of the state of public feeling with regard to the Bill and the majority in favour of the third reading had not been more than nine. Had the Bill been passed by a larger majority the Government would have felt it their duty to proceed with it. What Lord Liverpool omitted to say, however, was how delighted they were not to do so.

In the present state of the country and having regard to the nearly balanced division of opinion in the House the Government had decided not to proceed further with the Bill and he would now move that the question that "this Bill do now pass" should be amended to read, "that this Bill be now read this day six months," which, in parliamentary language, meant that the Bill was withdrawn.

This announcement, which appears to have taken many peers by surprise, was received with loud cheers and Lord Grey rose to speak but was unable to do so for some time because of the general confusion. When, at last, he was able to make himself heard, he charged the Government with gross neglect of duty in listening only to *ex parte* evidence and giving willing credence to the most exaggerated and unfounded calumnies. The Government had betrayed their King, Lord Grey said, insulted their Queen and shocked the morals of society by promulgating such detestable and disgusting evidence. He also blamed the Milan Commissioners. He was followed by Lord Erskine who said how happy he was to have lived to see justice done to the Queen, tardy and reluctant though it was.

Creevey, who had left the House of Lords immediately after the Prime Minister's announcement and dashed off to Brook's to celebrate, wrote from the club: "The Bill is gone thank God to the devil. Their majority was brought down to nine, and then the dolorous Liverpool came forward and struck. He moved that his own bill be read this day six months. You may well suppose the state we are all in . . . the state of the town is beyond everything."

SEVEN

Peace at Last

ᘓᘒ

THE WELCOME news first reached the public when someone threw open a window in the House of Lords and shouted, "The Bill is rejected," whereupon the crowd outside cheered like mad. By night time there were illuminations in Piccadilly, Bond Street and St. James's where there were celebrations in all the clubs. Crowds paraded through the streets carrying torches and shouting, "Long live Queen Caroline," and marched along keeping time with cries of "*Non mi ricordo, non mi ricordo.*"

On the following morning the Lord Mayor of London had a poster displayed in front of the Mansion House announcing that there would be illuminations in the City in honour of Her Majesty's triumph. Many houses were decorated with portraits of the Queen and Brougham and with posters proclaiming, among other things, that Caroline was still Regina.

Outside the auction rooms of Mr. Machin, which were brilliantly illuminated, there was a poster advertising that "In a few days will be submitted to public auction, if not previously disposed of, twenty-eight Elastic Consciences at all times devoted to their employer's wishes. For reference re character inquire at the office of the L−−d Chancellor. Further particulars may be had from the office of the secretary to the D−−− of N−wc−stle. May the Queen be protected from her enemies and the King be preserved from his pretended friends."

During the week following the withdrawal of the Bill the Queen's Vice-Chamberlain was instructed by her to apply to the Prime Minister for a "Palace suitable as the residence of the Queen of England" to be placed at her disposal without further delay. She received a curt reply stating that the King was not prepared to assign any of the royal palaces for her residence. Until Parliament reassembled, however, "the allowance hitherto enjoyed by the Queen would continue to be paid until the amount of future provision for Her Majesty had been determined." The Queen quite properly sent a long reply to the Prime Minister's letter on 18th November. As Parliament, which should have reassembled to do business on 23rd November was further prorogued to 23rd January the Queen made the contents of her letter public.

Written on her command by Mr. Craven, her Vice-Chamberlain, it began by stating that Her Majesty could not for a moment understand the real purport of Lord Liverpool's letter.

The Queen perceives that the King's Ministers have resolved to prevent Parliament from assembling for the despatch of business at the time to which both Houses had adjourned. The justice and wisdom of the legislature would at that period beyond all doubt have restored her to the full enjoyment of those rights which the constitution has vested in the Queen-Consort. The Ministers plainly show that such is their belief and they are determined, for some purposes of their own, to delay the redress to which she is entitled.

The letter then went on to say that the Queen saw behind all this something more sinister, namely that the authors of the Bill were trying to think out a new scheme to degrade her. "Defeated in their first attempt, disgraced in the eyes of the people, consigned to the contempt of all Europe, deserted by the most rational and respected of their own adherents, they meditate a new attack on the honour of the Queen."

If the Government really thought that any new scheme would be likely to succeed, the Queen felt sure that they were banking on the possibility that the public would get tired of supporting her as they had so loyally done in the past and that, perhaps, she also would give up the long struggle. She owed it to the British nation, the letter stated, to declare that she still had the utmost confidence in their support so long as she continued to be the victim of oppression, and no ill-treatment by the King's Ministers would ever shake the duty which she owed to the generous people who continued to stand up for her.

To the offer of money which the Prime Minister had thought proper to make when informing her of the further prorogation of Parliament she had no answer to give other than a direct refusal. The late King had been dead for nearly ten months, but no parliamentary provision had yet been made for her.

That public support for her had not yet wavered was evident from the numerous loyal addresses that poured in from all over the country as they had done, six months before, after the return of the Queen from abroad.

Caroline decided that it would be appreciated by the people, though not by the King or the Government, if she were to give thanks in public for what had been referred to as her "providential deliverance from her enemies and persecutors." Arrangements were, therefore, made for a service of thanksgiving in St. Paul's on Wednesday 29th November. The streets were lined with crowds of sympathizers and she was received at Temple Bar, on her way to the cathedral, by the Corporation.

The King did everything he could to make things difficult, but he could not barricade the streets through which the procession was to have passed for no one would have enforced the order had one been given, nor could he close the doors of the cathedral against her. He did, however, succeed in arranging that there should be no sermon by persuading the Dean and Chapter, who should not have been so weak and feeble, to give instructions to that effect. Nor was that all. The Dean also refused to allow a carpet to be laid from the West door through the nave and the choir to where the Queen's seat was situated, a remarkable example of Christian magnanimity. The pulpit and the lectern were not even allowed to be used for reading the lessons or any other purpose.

When the House of Commons met again after the recess an attempt was made by motions put down by Lord Archibald Hamilton and Mr. Wetherell to reinstate Caroline's name in the liturgy. They were moved during the debate on the King's speech, at the commencement of which Castlereagh had assured the House that no further measures of a hostile nature were intended towards Her Majesty and that a proposal would be submitted to the House for suitable provision to be made for her.

The attempt failed, however, for Hamilton's motion was defeated by 101 votes, but when the House was about to go into Committee to discuss financial provision for Her Majesty Brougham rose and said that he had the Queen's command to present the following message:

The Queen having learned that the House of Commons has appointed this day for taking into consideration that part of the King's most gracious speech which relates to her, deems it necessary to declare that she is duly sensible of His Majesty's condescension in recommending an arrangement respecting her to the attention of Parliament. She is aware that this recommendation must be understood as referring to a provision for the support of her estate and dignity; and from what has lately passed, she is apprehensive that such a provision may be unaccompanied by the possession of her rights and privileges in ample measure wherein former Queen-

Consorts, her Royal Predecessors, have been wont in times past to enjoy.

It is far from the Queen's inclination needlessly to throw obstacles in the way of a settlement which she desires in common with the whole country and which she feels persuaded the best interests of all parties equally require; and being most anxious to avoid everything that might create irritation, she cautiously abstains from any observation upon the unexampled predicament in which she is placed, but she feels it due to the House and to herself respectfully to declare that she perseveres in the resolution of declining any arrangement while her name continues to be excluded from the Liturgy.

The reading out of the Queen's message was greeted by loud and continued cheering and a lively and, at times, acrimonious debate took place, at the end of which a resolution that she should receive £50,000 per annum was agreed to without a division. Eventually, as she had debts to pay and had to have some income to live on, Caroline agreed to accept the sum voted without consulting Brougham.

Outside Parliament, however, the battle still went on and everything possible was done by the King and his clique to make life unbearable for the Queen. Some of the things done were described by Brougham in his autobiography:

Carlton House now took the course of filling the press with libels to deter all ladies from visiting the Queen. Papers were established with the avowed purpose of attacking every woman of rank who accepted her invitations. At the same time Carlton House was thrown open to such as refused to visit the Queen, and I hesitate not to declare that this course was perfectly successful, not merely with the women but also with their male relations so as, to my certain knowledge, to influence their votes in both the houses. Both were unwilling to expose their wives and sisters to a slanderous press, and averse to losing for them the balls at Carlton House.

The Queen bore it all with great patience and even good humour.

She used to say, "Oh it is all in the common course. People go to different inns: one goes to the King's Head, another to the Angel."

Brougham considered, however, that she did not act with discretion and that, although it would have been difficult to avoid making any mistakes in her peculiarly difficult position, she often invited the wrong people to visit her, people who came "for no other purpose than to gossip and laugh at her".

Life was not very pleasant for the Queen during these few weeks, for her attention was constantly being drawn to scandalous reports which appeared in the newspapers and which were purposely brought to her notice in the hope that she would become weary of it all and go abroad, which was what the King wanted, and quickly, before the coronation, when he rightly anticipated that there would be more trouble.

Caroline, however, had no intention of leaving England before the coronation, which it had now been decided would soon take place. Her claim was made to be crowned as a right and it was referred to the Privy Council and heard before a very crowded meeting at which Lord Harrowby was in the chair. The Law Officers attended and also present to advise were the Lord Chancellor, the Lord Chief Justice, the Chief Baron, and all the other judges who were Privy Councillors.

Brougham thus describes the meeting:

Denman and I argued the case for the claim, and Gifford and Copley against it and the decision was that as the Queen was living separate from the King she had no right to be crowned. Thus it was left to the King to refuse it.

This was manifestly a political judgment, entirely influenced by what had taken place the year before; for we showed by the clearest proofs that there was no instance whatever of a Queen not being crowned, except one when she was abroad, and another where there was a difference of religion and she declined it; but none whatever of a Queen-Consort not being crowned when she was within the realm, of the same religion as the King, and willing to be crowned.

My own impression was that the lay-Lords, not being in office— and even Lord Harrowby though in office—were inclined to our case, but that the Law Lords, including the judges, were against us— those judges who had taken a very decided part against us in the Lords as assessors to the House, and done themselves as little credit as possible in their answers to the legal question put to them, the most important of which has been disapproved by all lawyers since, and declared to be erroneous by late statutes—so much so that "the rule in the Queen's case" has been a strong topic of ridicule in the profession.

The hearing of the Queen's case to be crowned was heard on 4th July, and it was on that very day that the news first arrived in England that Napoleon had died on St. Helena on 6th May. Announcing the glad tidings to the King, his equerry said, "Your greatest enemy is dead, Sir." "Is she," said the King, his eyes glinting with joy and satisfaction, but his expression changed immediately when he was informed that it was not the Queen who was dead, but Bonaparte.

Realizing that Caroline was determined to appear in Westminster Abbey on the day of the coronation her legal advisers urged her strongly that it would be a great mistake to make the attempt. But it was useless: she had made up her mind.

It was not the first time that Caroline had committed errors of judgment, some of which she had probably regretted when it was too late, but there was nothing impetuous about this decision. She must have realized only too well that her attempt would, in all probability, fail, but she was determined to have one final fling and, having regard to all she had suffered during the past twenty-five years, who can blame her? Meanwhile, the King, who was not looking forward to his coronation and the scandal which it was likely to cause, had taken every precaution to prevent the

Queen reaching the Abbey. He had, however reserved a prominent seat for his present mistress Elizabeth, Lady Conyngham, who was frequently referred to as the Vice-Queen, and Sir Charles Bagot stated that while the King was kneeling at the altar, even during the Communion service, he repeatedly kissed a ring which had been given to him by Lady Conyngham.

Early on the day of the coronation Caroline left her house accompanied by Lady Hood and Lady Anne Hamilton, both of whom rode in the same carriage with her. In the other carriage were Lord Hood and her Vice-Chamberlain, Craven. The cortège was allowed to pass through the barrier which had been erected near the west door of the Abbey and eventually, after some confusion, her carriage drew up by the entrance and she approached the west door, leaning on the arm of Lord Hood. As they reached it the door was shut in her face. Lord Hood, having demanded entrance, the door keepers asked to see their tickets and the following conversation is reported to have taken place:

Lord Hood: "I present you your Queen, surely there is no need for her to have a ticket."

Door keeper: "Our orders are to admit no person without a Peer's ticket."

Lord Hood: "This is your Queen, she is entitled to admission without one."

The Queen: "Yes, I am your Queen, will you not admit me?"

Door keeper: "My orders are explicit and I must obey them."

Lord Hood: "I have a ticket."

Door keeper: "Then, my lord, we will let you pass if you will produce it."

Lord Hood then drew from his pocket a peer's ticket for one person, the original name had been erased and the name of Wellington had been substituted.

Door keeper: "This allows for the admission of only one person."

Lord Hood: "Will your Majesty go in alone?"

The Queen indicated that she would, but hesitated.

Lord Hood: "Am I to understand that you refuse her Majesty admission?"

Door keeper: "We have our orders."

Lord Hood: "Then you refuse the Queen admission?"

The Queen then decided to return to her carriage and, as she left the porch, some of the spectators laughed and hurled insults at her. She then went to the north entrance to the Abbey and was again refused admission.

Public opinion is forever changing, and the fickleness of the mob is proverbial. It is a question of "here today and gone tomorrow". Perhaps, being British, the crowd thought that she was a bad loser and felt that she should now take the lampooners' advice and "Go away at any rate". On this occasion she did, for in less than three weeks she was dead, and it can surely be said, whatever the medical diagnosis of her fatal illness was, that Caroline died of a broken heart.

This last indignity and insult which she had suffered must have been the more galling by reason of the fact that in her heart of hearts she knew that she had only herself to blame. Perhaps she realized this when she was first refused admission at the west door of the Abbey; but it was then too late, the damage had been done. She must secretly have cursed herself for her folly which had resulted in her being publicly insulted, as it were, in the face of the whole nation, and abroad as well, at a time when her credit and reputation had never stood so high.

As she drove back to her home she tried to conceal her chagrin from the crowds but she could not hide it from her friends. Nevertheless, they persuaded her to carry on as usual so as to prevent her ruminating too much on what had happened.

On Monday 30th July, therefore, although she was not feeling at all well Caroline kept a long standing engagement at Drury

Lane Theatre to see Edmund Kean in *Richard III*. Although she was taken ill during the performance she refused to leave until the end. On Tuesday she was slightly better, but the following day her doctor diagnosed a dangerous obstruction of the bowel. On Thursday and Friday she was still very ill though not considered to be in any danger.

Brougham was leaving that night for York and visited Caroline during the afternoon. "I was with her half an hour," he wrote. "She spoke calmly of her case and when I told her of the satisfactory opinion which I had just heard from her medical men she said, 'Oh no, my dear Mr. Brougham, I shall not recover and I am much better dead for I be tired of this life.'"

Stopping for the night at Grantham, on his journey to York, Brougham wrote and told Lord Grey, who, he was sure, "would be desirous of knowing really how the Queen was," for there were so many rumours going about. He added the following postscript to his letter: "I suppose the King would at first be very glad at her death, but he would soon find how odious it made him."

The Queen either knew that she was dying or was determined not to live if she could help it. When her leading physician, Dr. Holland, tried to tell her that her condition was still by no means hopeless all she said was, "No, my dear Sir, I fear your kind hopes will be disappointed."

By this time bulletins were being issued and none of them gave out much hope. On the Saturday morning it was rumoured that she had died at 7 a.m., and before it could be officially denied many tradesmen had closed their shops and some theatre managers sent messengers to Brandenburgh House to find out if it were true. At 3 p.m. the report was denied and Caroline was said to be improving slightly at which there was general relief which increased considerably when on Monday morning a still more favourable bulletin was issued, and on the Tuesday no bulletin at all.

But the improvement was only a flash in the pan and on 7th August, at 10.25 p.m., Caroline "passed peacefully away", having been unconscious for two hours.

As soon as the news reached York Brougham returned to London in order to attend the funeral and found that Lushington and Wilde (two of her counsel at the trial) had had a long interview with her before she died. She was then in no pain but she no longer knew what was going on around her or what she was saying, although she talked incessantly on almost every conceivable subject for three hours.

During her short but painful illness Caroline behaved with her usual courage and continually thought of others rather than of herself. All she wanted was to die. When her condition became worse Dr. Holland said that he would like a second opinion but, she said to him, "Do what you please if it will be any relief to your own mind, but do not do it for my sake. I have no wish to live: I would rather die." To one of her friends, who kept telling her that she would soon get well, she said, "Why do you wish me to live? Life to me can be nothing but a series of sorrows and persecution. I shall be much happier in another world than in this."

Speaking of her enemies she said that for years they had been conspiring and plotting to destroy her, and at last they had succeeded, but, "I forgive them. I die in peace with all mankind." She also sent for Mariette Bron, who was still in her service, and was the sister of Louisa Demont. She told Mariette that she forgave Demont for all her "cruel falsehoods".

When Wilde had visited her she added a codicil to her will. Her first wish had been to be buried in the same grave as her daughter Charlotte, but she said, "I can have little hope that the Government will grant me this wish. I desire, therefore, to be buried in the same vault with my father and mother in Brunswick."

Immediately after the Queen was dead Lushington wrote to the Earl of Liverpool giving him the news, and informing him that she had made a will and that he and Wilde were her executors. This letter the Prime Minister forwarded to the King and advised him to remain at Anglesey Castle, where he was staying, "until after the funeral which should be expedited as much as decency would permit." Unless the Queen had given any special direction in her will as to where she wished to be buried the Prime Minister suggested Windsor but, if the King objected to that, he suggested that she should be buried privately in Westminster Abbey.

The Prime Minister even thought it necessary to advise His Majesty of the "indispensable necessity of a mourning, as in no private family, whatever might have been the faults or sins of the individual, is mourning dispensed with." That he should have thought it necessary to give such advice to the King needs no comment. George was to be, if such a thing were possible, even more callous about his wife now that she was dead than he had been in her lifetime.

As soon as Lord Liverpool had seen Caroline's will, which was shown to him on the following day, he was able to tell the King that she had relieved him of all difficulties regarding her funeral by directing in her will that she was to be buried in Brunswick and that the coffin with her body should be sent off, if possible, within three days of her death.

In a second codicil to her will Caroline had directed that the inscription on her coffin should be, "Here lies Caroline of Brunswick, the injured Queen of England". The Prime Minister told the King that such an inscription would not be put on the coffin by authority or consent of the Government and Castlereagh agreed with this.

Meanwhile preparations for the lying in state were continued throughout Sunday and orders for ceremonial of the procession from London to Harwich were issued from the Lord Chamberlain's office. They stated that Her late Majesty's remains would be privately removed from Brandenburgh House on Tuesday morning at 7 a.m. and escorted by a squadron of the Royal Horse Guard via Romford to Chelmsford where they would be placed in the church under a military guard for the night. From there they would be taken via Colchester to Harwich for embarkation.

No mention was made, however, of the route which the procession would take after leaving Hammersmith, and inquiries were, therefore, made by the Sheriff of the County of Middlesex, in a letter to the Prime Minister asking for details to be given.

The following is an account which was given by Brougham who attended the funeral:

I took Sir Robert Wilson to Hammersmith where the Queen lay in state and from whence the procession took place. His son Henry, who had been one of her equerries, was in the carriage with us. The King had gone to Ireland, and Ministers having no orders, except to prevent all honours being paid and if possible to prevent the procession from marching through the city, acted upon their own notions of fulfilling his intentions and turned out the troops to obstruct our passage.

An attempt was made by us at Kensington to move round the palace and so reach Oxford street, as we were told that we must not go by Piccadilly. But they prevented us and obliged us to go through Hyde Park intending to turn us at Apsley House. We told them distinctly that the funeral must pass through the city. Nothing occurred till we got near Apsley House where the crowd was very great. The hearse was allowed to pass and was turned into the Park Lane direction by the soldiery. They then tried to stop us but we went on notwithstanding. I heard firing and one or two bullets whistled past us. On the first noise I asked Wilson what it was and he said "it is a noise you are not used to, we are under fire." Then said I, "We must get out of it but perhaps we should do so by going on." He said, "Certainly we should not be one whit worse than if we turned round." So we went forward. Only Wilson got out and told the officer commanding who we were and that we belonged to the procession. After a shot or two more this was effectual and we escaped without hurt, though one of the bullets struck the carriage. We then got into Oxford street and found it crowded by troops who made us turn into one of the streets leading to the New Road, the great object being to prevent us from getting into the city. However we made the procession go at a round pace so as to be there before the soldiery and this was the more easy because New Road was nearly empty, while the parallel streets were extremely crowded. We then got down the street that slants towards St. Paul's and were soon in the churchyard. The crowd was enormous and furious at the appearance of the soldiery.

As we moved slowly through it, several officers, not much liking their situation in the crowd, came up to our carriage and entered into conversation with us, manifestly thinking that their being seen to be friends would make things easier with the mob, which it did, for those officers were not at all maltreated, which the others were.

We at length got clear of the city, and went as far as Ilford in Essex on the Harwich road. We then returned to London . . . I was to start early next morning to overtake the funeral before it arrived at Chelmsford. I found it had just arrived and it was deemed proper that the coffin should be conveyed to the church, but the authorities there objected and Lushington had to call for the interposition of the magistrates to overcome the religious scruples of the clergy. Next morning it proceeded to Harwich at a continued rapid rate, these being the strictest orders sent from Dublin that the embarkation must be over before the arrival of the King which was fixed for the next day.

On arriving at Harwich we found everything ready prepared for immediate embarkation. The scene was such as I never can forget or reflect upon without emotion. The multitudes assembled from all parts of the country were immense, and the pier crowded with them as the sea was covered with boats of every size and kind, and the colours of the vessels were half-masted high, as on days of mourning. The contrast of a bright sun with the gloom on every face was striking, and the guns firing at intervals made a solemn impression.

One of the sights, however, which most struck me was a captain in the royal navy, who sat on the pier and could not be persuaded to leave it; he was deeply affected and wept exceedingly. Having been in her service and employed then and ever since in dispensing her charities, he could not tear himself away, but being refused his earnest request to accompany her remains to Brunswick, he was resolved to witness the embarkation.

The crimson coffin slowly descended from the pier and the barge that conveyed it bore the flag of England, floating over "Caroline of Brunswick, the murdered Queen of England!" (it was, in fact, the injured Queen) the inscription directed by herself, and the justice of which was felt by the thousands who had indignantly seen the indecent haste of the funeral procession from London, and who felt their share in a kind of national remorse, as well as commiseration for all that had passed.

What Brougham wrote about the public's instinctive feeling of disgust for the indecent haste with which Caroline's remains were bundled out of the country before the King returned from his holiday in Ireland was quite true. The cool reception which she had received from the crowd when she attempted to gate-crash the coronation proved to be short lived, and all the former sympathy for her and disdain for her royal husband came to life again as soon as the news of her illness became known. The final insult which the King offered to his Queen by trying to boycott· her last journey home from the country where she had encountered so much persecution roused the outraged mob to bitter anger.

The authorities were prepared for disturbances which they feared would take place along the route of the funeral procession and arrangements had been made by Sir Robert Baker, the chief magistrate at Bow street, to station police officers along the line of march to deal with such disturbances, and orders were also issued for the Household Cavalry to be on the alert in barracks in case of emergency. And they were needed, as riots broke out in many places when the troops tried to side-track the procession.

As the thousands who had gathered near the pier at Harwich saw the ship which carried the body of their injured Queen to its last resting-place disappear from sight, two thoughts were uppermost in their minds; a feeling of relief that all her suffering was now a thing of the past, and of revulsion for their Sovereign who had been the cause of it all.

In his book, *The Modern British Monarchy*, Sir Charles Petrie states that our monarchy in its modern form, that is to say, accepted and respected, dates from the reign of Queen Victoria, and that what it was before that is admirably summed-up in the well-known lines of Walter Savage Landor:

> I sing the Georges four,
> For Providence could stand no more.
> Some say that far the worst
> Of all the four was George the First.
> But yet by some 'tis reckoned,
> That worse still was George the Second.
> And what mortal ever heard,
> Any good of George the Third?
> When George the Fourth from earth descended,
> Thank God the line of Georges ended.

Index

Index

Index

Hyatt, Admiral, 121

J

Jason, H.M. Frigate, 62, 63
Jersey, Lady, 13, 16–17, 21 n., 24, 141

K

Karlsruhe, 124
Kean, Edmund, 159
Kempshott, 19
Kensington, 47, 50, 53
Kent, Duke of, 28–9
Kenyon, Lord, 87–8
King, Lord, 109–10, 114
Kress, Barbara, 124, 125, 127

L

Lancing, 61, 62
Landor, Walter Savage, 165
Lansdowne, Lord, 138
Lauderdale, Earl of, 145–6
Lawrence, Sir Thomas, 35
Leach, Sir John, 68, 123
Leinster, Duke of, 105
Lindsay, Lady Charlotte, 58–60, 62, 136
Liverpool, Lord, 70–2, 78–9, 82, 86–9, 98, 100–1, 103, 105, 131–3, 138–9, 148, 149, 151, 160–1
Lloyd, Frances, 36
Louise of Mecklenberg-Strelitz, Princess, 14
Lushington, Mr., 160–1

M

McCarthy, Justin, 52
Machin, Mr., 150
Macirone, Count, 64–5
Majocchi, Theodore, 114–22, 126, 130, 133, 137, 143–4, 145
Malmesbury, James Harris, Earl of, 9, 14, 15–17, 19–20

Manby, Captain, 35, 43
Marsh, John, 121
Matthew, General Montague, 64
Maule, Mr., 115
Melville, Lord, 72
Mercer, Miss, 60
Milan, 65, 112, 116
  Conference, 68–9, 79, 92, 123, 138, 139, 149
Monroe, Colonel, 75
Montague House, Blackheath, 24–34 *passim*, 36, 37, 40, 46, 50, 115
Mont St. Gothard, 112
Morning Chronicle, 49
Munster, Count, 66

N

Naples, 64–5, 110, 112, 137
Napoleon Bonaparte, 156
Norfolk, Duke of, 104
Nottingham, 104

O

Ompteda, Baron, 66–8
Orange, Prince of, 19, 57–8

P

Pains and Penalties, Bill of, 50, 65, 81, 96, 99
  prosecution, 100–131
  defence, 131–46
  division, 146
  amendments, 147
  end of, 148–9, 150
Parry, Sir Edward, 12
Pechell, Captain, 122–3
Peel, Robert, 140
Perceval, Spencer, 40, 45, 46, 47–8
Perdita, *see* Robinson, Mary
Pergami, Baron, 65, 66, 110–13, 115, 116, 119, 121, 123–4, 125–7, 130, 137, 147

Index